COACHING FOOTBALL'S POLYPOTENT OFFENSE

COACHING FOOTBALL'S POLYPOTENT OFFENSE

RICHARD T. BARAN

Parker Publishing Company, Inc. • West Nyack, N.Y.

©1974 by

Parker Publishing Company, Inc.
West Nyack, N.Y.

Library of Congress Cataloging in Publication Data

Baran, Richard T
   Coaching football's polypotent offense.

   1. Football—Offense. 2. Football coaching.
I. Title.
GV951.8.B37   796.33'212   74-4074
ISBN 0-13-139055-4

Printed in the United States of America

To Cheryl and Lisa, my daughters,
whom I love more
than anything else in the world

How the Polypotent Offense
Can Help You

What is the Polypotent Offense? It is an offense of many, varied strengths. It is first a system of play-calling that abandons the traditional numbering system and uses the *language* of football. A powerful, explosive offense, the Polypotent Offense employs flexible, yet simplified and easy-to-learn, blocking assignments.

This offense has been proved in championship play, and it also gives a coach the needed leverage to lift average teams into contention. The Polypotent Offense features several forces going for it at all times. It offers a ball control ground game, while having available a wide open passing attack that is discussed in Chapter 6. Chapter 2 presents a new concept of the "Belly Series" with a companion triple-option play.

Your entire team will like this offense. A great amount of pride and morale can be developed by your linemen with the Polypotent Offense because they know that they are prepared to handle any situation that comes up during the course of the game. They are given the job of calling their blocks and adjustments, for example, at the off-tackle hole by using "exception" blocking as described in Chapter 4.

Why the Polypotent Offense? Each year at football clinics, smokers, and bull sessions, thousands of X's and O's are scrawled, manipulated, and maneuvered by high school coaches who have optimistic hopes of success. Humanity reduced to two letters—X and O—is programmed for the coming autumn games. But what is the outcome of these master-minded blueprints? What happened to the "Veer" and the "Wishbone" and the "Pro-shift" after they appeared on secondary school fields? What went wrong in the transfer from paper to stadium? One possible answer is fundamentals. More and more coaches are rationalizing time away from basics and allocating it to teach the complexities of some new offense. In Chapter 9, you'll see the methods of teaching blocking fundamentals in the Polypotent Offense, along with functional and game-condition drills which are used to conserve practice time. Another possible answer could be the breakdown in the process of the coach communicating his knowledge, not only to his players but to his assistants. This area is one of the basic building blocks of the offensive system and is discussed in Chapter 1, along with the descriptive terminology for the Polypotent Offense. The methods of applying these terms for the various blocks are then incorporated for you into an effective communication system in play calling.

The Polypotent Offense can help you win more football games. It can make for a more successful program at your school regardless of enrollment. And, above all, it can make your athletes better football players and you a better coach. *Coaching Football's Polypotent Offense* offers not only the basic system from a step-by-step approach, but it also goes into detail by discussing various coaching points, line and backfield techniques, and strategies with each play mentioned. Many of the fine points of any system are often times hurried over or eliminated at clinics and lectures. These are the same details that are responsible for the success of a particular play which does not come off the way you want it on the field. *Coaching Football's Polypotent Offense* goes into the areas of backfield footwork, adjusted line spacing, variations in alignment and rules for every play. It is these same fine points which make it easier for the system, as a whole or in part, to be adopted into your offensive system.

R.T.B.

ACKNOWLEDGMENTS

I would like to acknowledge the following:

Mr. Emil Stubits, *Chicago Sun-Times*. His help got me in the door.

Mr. Joseph Sassano, Assistant Director, Athletic and Convocation Center, University of Notre Dame and, former Head Football Coach, Weber High School, Chicago, Illinois. He made me a better football coach and his ideas influenced the theory in this book.

Weber High School, Chicago, Illinois, and its players and coaches from 1963-1967. Here was football at its finest and memories that will never die.

The members of the Chicago League Coaches Association past, present, and future. They will always know the true meaning of dedication and comradery.

Many thanks to my coaching colleagues at Wheeling High School, Wheeling, Illinois, especially Dennis W. Toll, whose genuine loyalty I will never forget.

A special thank you to Perry Guedry for his constructive criticism of my writing.

A Special Thanks

I would like to take this opportunity to thank three fine gentlemen for giving me the chance to share my football thoughts with my fellow coaches through their fine publications.

Mr. John L. Griffith, Publisher, *Athletic Journal*, for his cooperation and assistance in the use of his sequence photographs for some of the demonstrations.

Mr. Herman L. Masin, Editor, *Scholastic Coach*, for both his acceptance and constructive rejection of my efforts.

Mr. Dwight Keith, Editor, *Coach & Athlete*, for publishing my material.

CONTENTS

COACHING FOOTBALL'S POLYPOTENT OFFENSE

CHAPTER 1

Descriptive Terminology for
Running the Polypotent Offense

THE PSYCHOLOGY OF COMMUNICATION
IN FOOTBALL

Your staff meeting was a picture of corporate efficiency. Ideas were formulated and conveyed. Plans were drafted and okayed. Authority was delegated. Optimism ran high. Talent and experience seemed to be in abundance. Practice went according to schedule. The competition didn't have a prayer. Then the scoreboard flashed the final results and you began to wonder what went wrong.

Assuming the clarity of communication was no problem for the staff, examine another possible area for the unexpected breakdown. Whom are you attempting to coach? With what type of individuals are you working? Who's to receive the benefit of your athletic knowledge and experience? In the majority of cases, it is the adolescent—that strange, bewildered, functioning organism between ages 13 and 19 who finds himself, for one reason or another, in athletic activities that so closely parallel the good times and bad, the joys and sorrows, and the ups and downs of life. So, what does this have to do with coaching? What does this have to do with the process of having players execute those carefully-drafted plans under the pressure of competition?

In looking at the area of communication, two problems are fairly obvious. One is that we are human and being so we have been known to misunderstand and to make mistakes. The other problem is forgetting that others are human, too. If our players were robots, there would be no difficulty. They would accept our coaching without question and put it into efficient action. Our mechanical jocks would have no pre-existing attitudes which might conflict with our ideas. They would have no emotions to distract them, no secrets to keep, and no egos to be fed. However, there are no robots in athletics. It is the human element which attempts to channel its efforts toward a goal and success.

The communication process guides a team along the road to success. Whether it be in the actual practice instruction or the inaugural team meeting with its presentation of training rules and regulations, or handling individual problems as the season progresses, the positive responses of a particular person or group have to be affected. There must be understanding and acceptance in this verbal exchange. Without them, there is no communication.

Meaning to anything is found in people. We know that no two people are alike and that no two people can ever find exactly the same meaning for anything. Ask yourself how each member of your team interpreted your training rules. At the time they were presented, it appeared that all eyes in the room focused on you. It was evident that you had their undivided attention. But, did you get that positive response? Did you get the desired results? Were your rules followed? Were they effective?

MISUNDERSTANDING LOSES TOO MANY GAMES

How many times has a play been sent into a game from the sidelines only to have the wrong formation called, or the wrong block thrown, or the wrong pattern run, or an extirely different play carried out for a loss? It happens all the time. How often has the ambiguous shout, "Block someone!" echoed from the sidelines? Sure, "someone" is blocked. But, was he the right one? Was he taken the right way? Was the proper technique used? Was there a gain?

The coach and his staff who can communicate with their team during the confusion of a game will come out the winner. Adjustments and regrouping can be accomplished during half time and many teams play superb football during the third and fourth quarters. However, corrections must also be made during the game. A coaching staff that paces the sidelines during the game only kills grass. Instead, they should be trying to pick up what the opponent is doing differently from what had been anticipated and get this information to their players. The rules, in some form or another, allow coaching from the sidelines, sending in plays or instructions, and communicating with a player during timeouts. It is in these short sessions where many games are won. The coach can't be on the field with his players and the only way he can help them is if they know without a doubt what he is trying to get across to them.

FEWER MISTAKES THROUGH COMMUNICATION

In order for cram sideline coaching instructions to be effective there has to be communication. For any exchange between player and coach to be of any value, a uniform set of terms has to be installed into the entire football program. It must be a system, a way of talking in terminology familiar to the entire staff and to every player. Each term must have a specific meaning and that meaning should bring about the desired response. Instead of shouting, "Block!" to a player, the proper execution of a play could be brought about by calling out, "Shut-Off!" "Watchdog!" would have the necessary meaning. "Chop-in" or "Closedown" have the meanings understood by both player and coach. The important thing is that the chances of misunderstanding are reduced by decription and communication.

TERMINOLOGY FOR THE POLYPOTENT OFFENSE

There are those who might not agree with the concept of offense by semantics but, it has won football games and will continue to do so. At first, some of the terms might seem simple and obvious. To the coach, yes. The player is a different story. He is learning the game which you have made a career. He must learn and you must teach. He must understand and execute and you must coach.

As the definitions unfold, the descriptive concept will crystallize and the Polypotent Offense will take shape. It will soon become apparent that no numbers are used. The terms to be learned start out as follows:

Inside: Toward the center.

Outside: Away from the center. See Diagram 1-1.

Front side: The side where the ball is going.

Back side: The side away from the ball. See Diagram 1-2.

Gap: The space between offensive linemen. See Diagram 1-3.

Split: The distance offensive linemen will spread from each other. The basic line "splits" are 1 foot, 2 feet, and 3 feet from center to guard, guard to tackle and tackle to end. Variations to this rule depend on the play being run and the individual player's ability for quick lateral movement. For example, on inside plays a maximum split is desired to create better blocking angles and/or to widen the running lane.

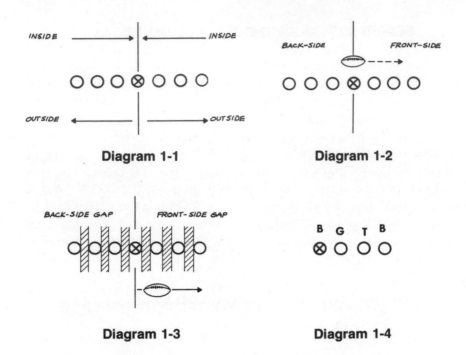

Diagram 1-1   **Diagram 1-2**

Diagram 1-3   **Diagram 1-4**

On: Defensive man on or off the line who lines up on any part of the offensive man. See Diagram 1-4.

In: Defensive man on or off the line from the offensive man's inside gap to head up the next offensive lineman. See Diagram 1-5.

Out: Defensive man on or off the line from the offensive man's outside gap to head up the next offensive lineman. See Diagram 1-6.

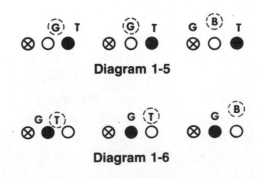

Diagram 1-5

Diagram 1-6

Shoulder: A defensive man lined up on the inside or outside shoulder. He is still classified as "On" but the term "shoulder" is used in designating certain blocking assignments. See Diagram 1-7.

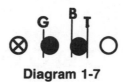

Diagram 1-7

THE TYPES OF BLOCKS

Continuing with establishing operational definitions, names are assigned to each of the blocks that will be used in the Polypotent Offense. The theory driven home here is that the blockers are trying to create a running lane for the ball carrier. The blockers can accomplish this by fighting for body position or they can utilize blocking angles to create an inside and outside wall for the lane. See Diagrams 1-8 (a) and (b). In

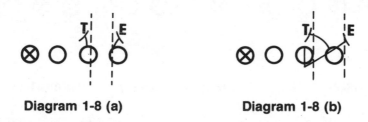

Diagram 1-8 (a)   **Diagram 1-8 (b)**

Chapter 9, instructional techniques and drills will be taken up for developing the blocks which are:

Zone: A shoulder block to the man "On" trying to turn him away from the play. The "Zone" term is also a blocking call which is discussed in Chapter 4. See Diagram 1-9.

Crackdown: A block on the first man "In" using the near shoulder and putting the head behind. The expression, "Inside shoulder" is also used in place of "In" for some assignments. See Diagram 1-10.

Diagram 1-9   **Diagram 1-10**

Closedown: A block on the first man "In" using the far shoulder. The head is put in front of the defender in an effort to prevent his penetration. "Inside shoulder" pertains also to this block. See Diagram 1-11.

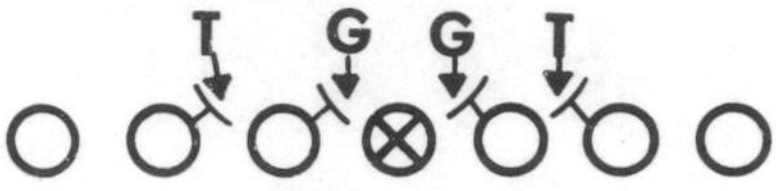

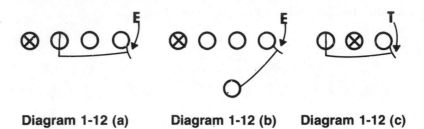

Diagram 1-11

Kick-out: A running shoulder block on a man to the "Outside." The blocker follows the rule: Kick-out right use the right shoulder. Kick-out left use the left shoulder. The outside portion of the "running lane," in many cases, is established by the "Kick-out." See Diagrams 1-12 (a) (b) (c).

Diagram 1-12 (a)   Diagram 1-12 (b)   Diagram 1-12 (c)

Shut-off: A block on the first man "In" to fill for a pulling lineman and to prevent penetration. The offensive man slides laterally, keeping his shoulders parallel to the line of scrimmage. See Diagram 1-13. This is also illustrated in Chapter 9.

Diagram 1-13

Scramble: The term applied to a four-point crab technique used by the blocker to help him keep contact and avoid falling to the ground.

Chop-in: A running cross-body block on a man to the "outside." The blocker must aim for the outside leg, work to get his head and shoulders pointing upfield to the goal line, and "scramble. See Diagrams 1-14 (a) and (b)

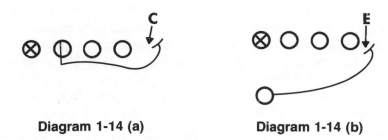

Diagram 1-14 (a)   **Diagram 1-14 (b)**

Watchdog: A "crackdown" block on a linebacker to the "inside." See Diagrams 1-15 (a) and (b)

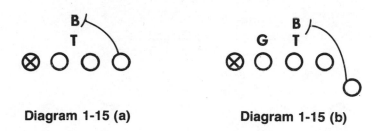

Diagram 1-15 (a)   **Diagram 1-15 (b)**

Lead: A running shoulder block at the area of attack usually thrown by a backfield man. The purpose of the "Lead" is twofold. First, it is designed for a one-on-one collision with a linebacker and second, the lead back can help a lineman with his block or pick up a linebacker scraping down the line. See Diagram 1-16 (a) (b).

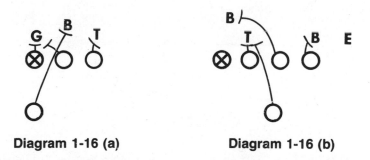

Diagram 1-16 (a)   **Diagram 1-16 (b)**

POLYPOTENT BLOCKING CALLS

Terms have been applied to the fundamental blocks of football. Nothing fancy. Nothing complicated. Meaning and understanding, however, now pertain to the basics of the game. Here, more than anywhere, is where the most frequent breakdowns have occurred. The next logical step is to apply these terms for the various blocks and incorporate them into an effective communication system in play calling. Each player associates one type of block with a particular type of play-action call. These play-action calls refer to the type of blocking which will be used at the area the offense plans to attack. They are explained and diagrammed as follows:

Power: A kick-out by a back at the point of attack, accompanied by the tackle and end to the front side using zone and crackdown blocks respectively. The end's crackdown could result in a double-team block or his scraping by the tackle's zone block and "watchdogging" on the linebacker. See Diagram 1-17. Also, Diagram 3-35.

"X": Cross blocking between two adjacent linemen, utilizing the crackdown and the kick-out. See Diagram 1-18.

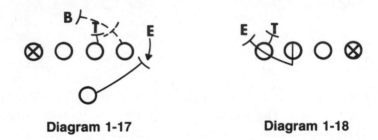

Diagram 1-17   Diagram 1-18

"Belly: A kick-out block by the front side guard, with the front side tackle and end using crackdown blocks. See Diagram 1-19. Also, Chapter 2 on the "Belly" series.

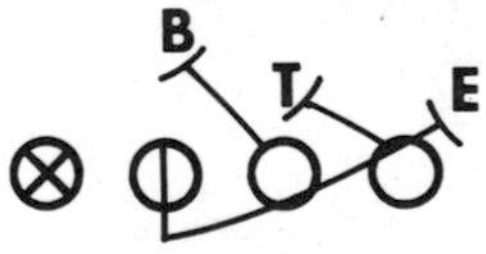

Diagram 1-19

"Fin" and "Fo": Fold- or step-through blocking is a partial crossing action used by the guard and tackle or tackle and end. It creates better angles and routes to cut off linebackers. "Fo" or fold blocking by the guard and tackle is a crackdown by the tackle and a short pull "out" with a "lead" up through by the guard. The term "Fo" refers to the action of the inside lineman in the combination. He is moving to his outside to carry out the fold block. Neither man waits for the other. On the count, they're moving. The inside man uses a drop-step action which gives the tackle in this example enough time to clear before the guard steps around. See Diagram 1-20 (a). "Fin" is the blocking combination for the End and Tackle. It literally means a fold-type of block coming from the outside man to be put on a defender to the inside. The tackle kicks-out and the end steps to the inside and through to cut off the linebacker. Again, neither man waits for the other. The drop-step action by the end gives the tackle a chance to clear so a collision is avoided. See Diagram 1-20 (b).

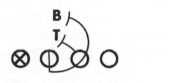 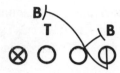

Diagram 1-20 (a): "Fo"   **Diagram 1-20 (b): "Fin"**

Sweep: Both guards pull to the front side. The sweep will be discussed and analyzed in Chapter 5. See Diagram 1-21.

Diagram 1-21

Trap: A crackdown-crackdown combination by the center and front-side guard with a kick-out by the back-side guard. See Diagram 1-22. Also, see Chapter 3 which covers the short interior trap and counter-trapping game.

Zone: The front-side linemen fire out and block the men "on". See Diagram 1-23.

Bootleg: The back-side guard pulls to the front side to protect the quarterback on a pass or to chop-in at the corner on a run. See Diagram 1-24.

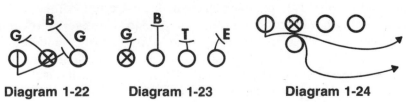

Diagram 1-22   **Diagram 1-23**   **Diagram 1-24**

BACKFIELD TERMS
AND FORMATION CALLS

The backfield positions are designated for the football purist. No 1's, 2's, 3's or 4's. Instead, Quarterback, Halfback, Fullback, Wingback, I-Back, Slotback and Flanker. Their alignments may vary for a particular play, but basically the halfback splits the inside of his tackle and is about three and one-half yards off the ball. The fullback is four yards off the ball and the I-Back is one-half to one yard behind the fullback. He is in a two-point stance while the other set backs are grounded in a three-point. The slotback and the wingback are a yard outside and a yard deep and do not angle in. The flanker's split is 10-12 yards but will shorten down if he has any blocking-back assignments to the inside. See Diagram 1-25.

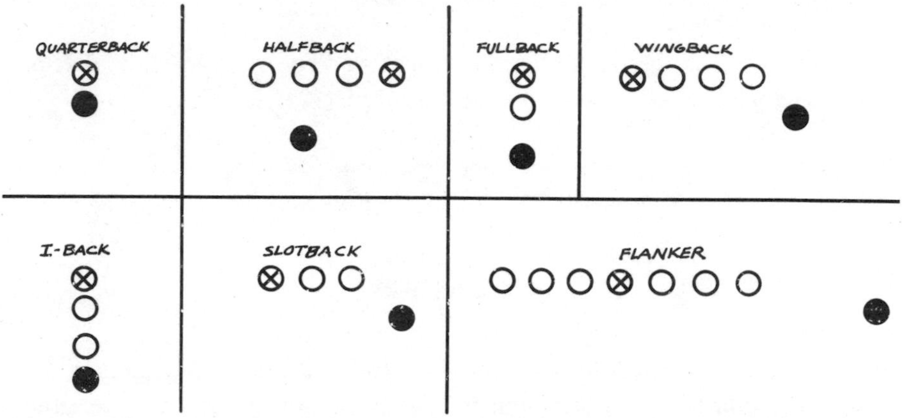

Diagram 1-25

Formations are also assigned universal football meanings. The number and types of sets used depend on many things ranging from practice time, to strategy, to the mental capabilities of the players. A particular game or defense may dictate certain splits. A shift or man-in-motion can be employed to attack a certain defensive set. Formations, of course, don't win football games. The players do. However, formations have a say-so in what can be done successfully by better utilizing the talent of the players. Some typical formations and their calls are illustrated in Diagram 1-26. The "T" and "I" are set up without the ends because of the multiple variations available.

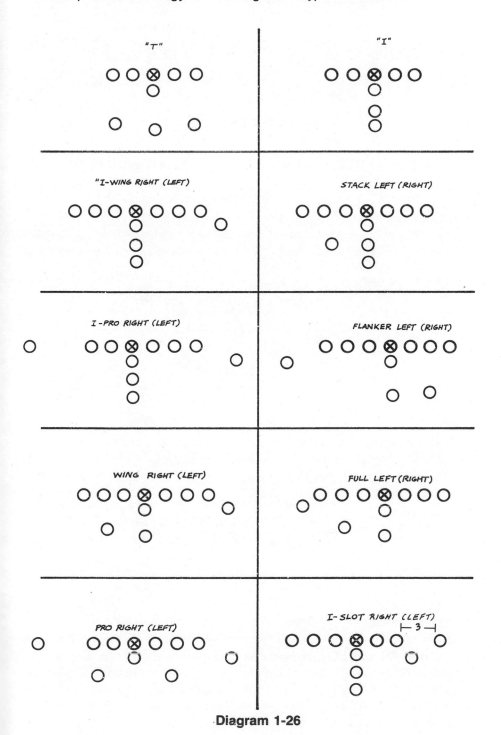

Diagram 1-26

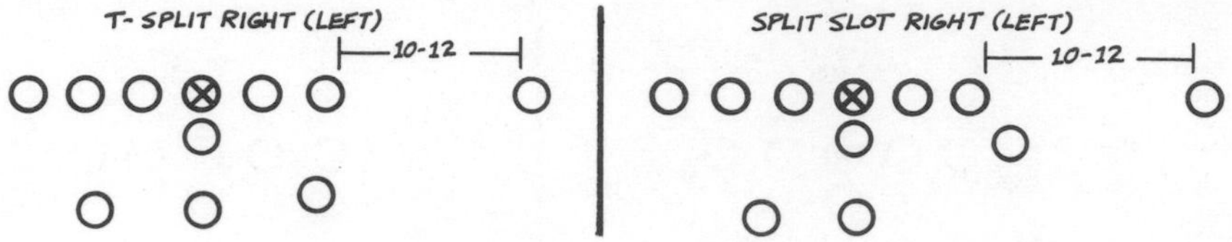

T- SPLIT RIGHT (LEFT)   SPLIT SLOT RIGHT (LEFT)

Diagram 1-26 (continued)

POLYPOTENT PLAY CALLS WITHOUT NUMBERS

Most of us were indoctrinated into offensive football under the number system of calling plays. When drawing up an offense, just about any coach will assign numbers to running areas and backfield positions as shown in Diagram 1-27. As players, there were a few coaches who had

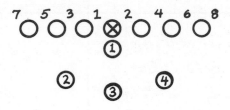

Diagram 1-27

trouble keeping in mind odd numbers to the left and even numbers to the right. They set up their own variations in numbering as shown in Diagram 1-28. Other coaches began to break with tradition by analyzing and alter-

Diagram 1-28

ing the numbering of holes. Being more realistic, they felt that if a defender lined up in a seam of the running lane or area the play would be hindered. By widening the holes, as shown in Diagram 1-29, they devised a more flexible approach. Other innovations have been incorporated into play calling by adding descriptive words for such plays as traps, counters, and passes. Sometimes, almost unknowingly coaches have abandoned the numbers. For example, they might instruct their teams in short-yardage situations to line up in a tight formation and run some type of straight ahead play which they'll call "Wham" or "Tear."

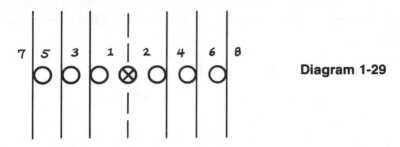

Diagram 1-29

Formations have also been assigned numbers as the digits add up. And all of this totals up to a deciphering of codes by the players as they break from the huddle and prepare to carry out their assignments, or possibly do their mathematics homework. To illustrate, a situation is used where the quarterback calls: "400-128 Power Sweep on 3." In Diagram 1-30, the quarterback, No. 1, hands off to the halfback, No. 2, who runs the eight hole from a 400 formation which has the No. 4 back on the right wing.

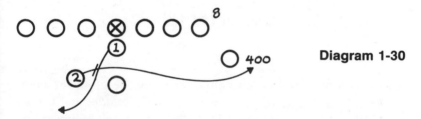

Diagram 1-30

As mentioned, there are no backs numbered in the Polypotent Offense. Nor are the holes numbered or lettered along the line of scrimmage. The slide rule has been retired and the language of football has taken its place. In the Polypotent Offense, the sweep play in Diagram 1-30 is called Wing Right-Sweep Right—no mathematical translations. Any number of series of plays can be drawn up by applying the strict word concept. A detailed explanation of the no-number, descriptive Polypotent Offense is given in Chapters 2-8.

THE POLYPOTENT HUDDLE AND CADENCE

Two final areas covered here are the huddle and the snap cadence. The huddle is illustrated in Diagram 1-31. This type of huddle, with the quarterback facing his bench, offers the following advantages: First, the quarterback can always see substitutes coming into the game. Second, it is easier to read any hand signals which might be flashed from the coach. Third, it is easier for the crossing of personnel if you are flip-flopping your line.

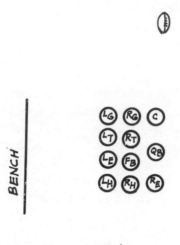

Diagram 1-31

When the quarterback finishes calling the play, he gives the command, "Center." At this time, the center leaves the huddle and has an extra second or two for any possible adjustments which might have to be made with the ball. "Ready—Break" brings the team up to the line.

The cadence is non-rhythmic and starts with the quarterback calling "Set" to ground his linemen. If an audible or blocking call is used, it is inserted at this point. "Ready" is the preparatory command and the execution takes place on the word, "Hit." The ball can be snapped on "Set," "Ready," or the first through the fourth "Hit." During practice or pre-practice, quarterbacks should work on varying the snap count as well as changing the volume of their voice on long counts. The long count, however, is dropped near the goal line or on short-yardage plays where being cute might get your own people jumping offside.

The meaning of every word used by a football team in its mode of operation is extremely important. The limited time element in the huddle places even more emphasis on communication. Therefore, every term used in offensive play calling must have a definite, explicit meaning.

CHAPTER 2

Developing the Belly Series
in the Polypotent Offense

"BELLY"

Eliminating the numbers from the Polypotent Offense does not create the obvious problems which first come into mind. Where is the play run? What hole? Who carries the ball? Players are shown this through the old familiar coaching-teaching process. They are given a concept and a theory and through practice, repetition, and study, the where, what, and who are reinforced.

The "Ride," "Drive," or "Belly" Series was originally based on an inside fake to the fullback followed by a quarterback keep-pitch option at the corner. An inside series was also developed. By adapting and expanding the Belly-blocking rule, with its front-side guard-out concept (See Diagram 1-19), to the Belly Series and adding one other play, the Polypotent Offense operates a strong, versatile basic ground attack. It is a series where every area along the line is hit with the varied use of one blocking rule: "Belly." The front-side guard knows he always has an out block and, in most cases, the tackle and end to the front side have crackdown assignments.

THE POLYPOTENT BELLY BLAST

Advocates of a strong running game insist that the off-tackle area is the focal point for success. In no way is this refuted. Control the off tackle with a cloud of dust and the game is yours. To help gain this important piece of dirt, a strong inside play is added to the Belly Series in the

Polypotent Offense to complement the off-tackle and option plays. The "Belly Blast" involves the I-Back following his fullback on a play which can open from the center's front-side gap to the tackle's nose. See Diagram 2-1. In calling the basic series, "Belly" is both the backfield maneuver and the blocking. "Blast" is the I-Back's inside play.

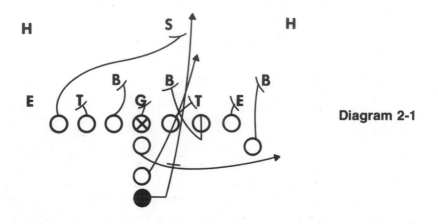

Diagram 2-1

Line splits for the front-side guard and tackle can be opened up to two and one-half four feet. This varies, more or less, with the quickness of the individual linemen in carrying out their objective of creating a running lane. Splits to the backside are normal or even cut down if penetration is a problem and the back-side players are made inside-gap conscious. Any possible penetration to the front side should be handled by the fullback in carrying out his "lead" responsibility.

The fullback lines up in a three-point stance three and one-half yards from the ball. The I-Back is about one yard behind him in a two-point stance. The fullback leads and reads taking his first step with his foot to the front side. He aims for the center's front-side hip and starts looking for penetration. If no one shoots, he follows the block of the front-side guard and cleans up the running lane. He does not waste himself if the blocks are being sustained but, continues to escort his ball carrier "to the goal line."

The I-back's footwork starts with a lateral step to the side of the play. From there, he pushes off and follows his fullback trying to read the path of the guard. His shoulders are always parallel to the line and that includes the initial lateral step.

Assignments for the front-side guard, tackle, and end do vary from the basic Belly idea, but the guard does block out and the tackle in. The front-side guard kicks-out on the first man lined up ''on'' the tackle who is on the line. The front-side tackle drop-steps with his inside foot, steps up through, and blocks the first man lined up ''on'' to inside the guard on or off the line. A zone block is needed from the front-side end to eliminate the chance of any defender squeezing in hard from the out-side.

If the defense would always cooperate there would be no need for adjustments in the blocking scheme. However, if the defensive tackle moves to his inside, the guard's block becomes much more difficult. Therefore, a rule revision is necessary. The ''Fo'' call between the guard and tackle on the ''Blast'' creates a better angle and makes available greater flexibility against blocking multiple defensive sets. See Diagrams 2-2 and 2-3. It also puts to better use the fullback's lead block.

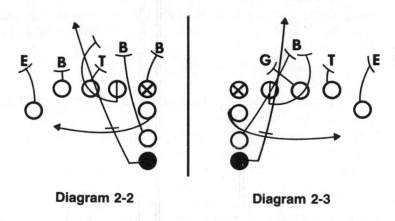

Diagram 2-2   **Diagram 2-3**

The quarterback's footwork is most important on the ''Blast.'' See Diagram 2-4. In coaching the quarterback, it has to be stressed that if the second step goes more than half way, he will cut off his fullback's course

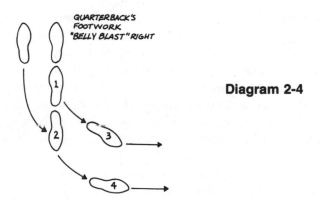

QUARTERBACK'S
FOOTWORK
"BELLY BLAST" RIGHT

Diagram 2-4

and force him too wide to be of any help in picking up a defender who has shot the center-guard gap. Step No. 1 is a short, backward jab to loosen the foot for the start of the pivot. The handoff is made on the third step.

A sample of the assignment sheet for the "Belly Blast" in the Polypotent Offense would read as follows:

> *Back-side End:* Downfield.
>
> *Back-side Tackle:* Zone.
>
> *Back-side Guard:* Front-side gap, zone.
>
> *Center:* Front-side gap, zone, back-side gap.
>
> *Front-side Guard:* Kick-out the man head up the Tackle on the line. "Fo" rule: First linebacker inside out.
>
> *Front-side Tackle:* Step through and block the first man on to inside your Guard. "Fo" rule: Crackdown from your inside shoulder to head up the Guard.
>
> *Front-side End:* Zone.

Diagrams for the play and the "Fo" blocking variations would also be included on the assignment sheet.

Any I-formation set can be used for the Blast as long as the play is run to the side of three blockers up front, i.e. tight end or slot back. As for any communicating on the line, the back-side linemen should make their own false calls to wipe out any chance of a tip-off. The center will make his own "Front-side!" call as his own oral reminder to check the front-side gap first in carrying out his assignment. He makes his call between the "Set" and "Ready" portion of the cadence.

DRILLS FOR THE BLAST

In discussing practice or drills, one important area should be covered. It is a good idea always to place a man "on" your center. Whether it's pre-practice, signal drills, punts, dummy, or live, the center should always have someone giving him a shot so that he never forgets that his second job is to block. Snapping the ball 25-or-so times to the quarterback before practice is great for the exchange. Snapping the ball 25-or-so times before practice with a defender using a dummy to play games with your center's nose is even greater. It will make your center a better football player.

The Blast is easy to teach. For those with the small, two-man staff, this play is easily broken down into two units for instruction. Diagrams

2-5 and 2-6 illustrate skeleton work for these groups. Here is where the play is made. Run standard defenses against it. Run your opponent's defenses against it. Run off-sets or stunt it to death. Try to get your players to recognize what is happening and to apply their rules in all situations. Stress the importance to the ball carriers of knowing the over-all play so that they are aware of, not only who is blocking for them, but also where the blocks are coming from so that they can get a quicker picture of the running lane developing.

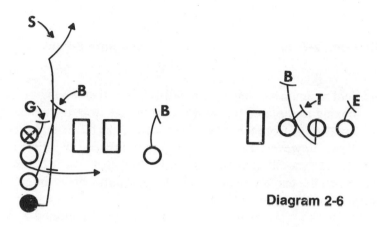

Diagram 2-6

Diagram 2-5

THE POLYPOTENT BELLY SLANT

The true belly blocking rule is used here as the series moves to the off-tackle area. Where "Blast" had a definite meaning to the linemen and backs, "Belly Slant" also designates backfield action, line blocking, and the point of attack. See Diagrams 2-7 (a) and (b) for the Belly Slant. The play can be run from an I-set or a conventional halfback-fullback align-ment. It gives the running back a shot at the off-tackle hole and also sets up the belly version of the triple option from almost the same action. Belly blocking rules are followed by the linemen to the front side of the play with the end using a crackdown on the first man to his inside who is on the line. If there is no man on the line, then he picks up the linebacker inside. The front-side tackle uses a crackdown on the first man to his inside while the front-side guard looks for the first man lined up head-on to outside the end on the line. He uses a kick-out.

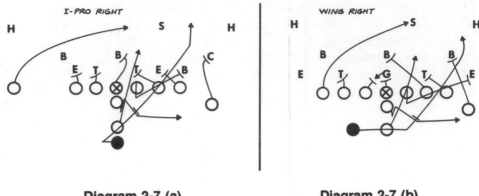

Diagram 2-7 (a)   **Diagram 2-7 (b)**

    Backfield assignments have the near back, whether a wing or a lead halfback, looking to the area for the first linebacker from the inside out. He must be sealed off from the play. The fullback has the exact footwork from the Blast. However, he must take a ride fake as he fills for the pulling guard. He should also be constantly reminded that it is his fake which can make the end's crackdown a more effective block in creating the inside wall of the running lane.

    The footwork for the quarterback is illustrated in Diagram 2-8. With proper timing, the hand-off should come with the fourth step. The quarterback then continues on with a keep fake. If, by chance, he misses the exchange, then he should cut up behind his back and follow him through the hole. This is true of any play where there is a missed handoff. Several

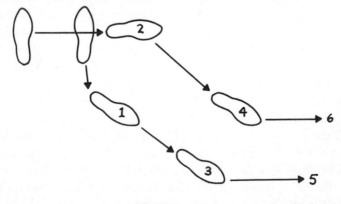

Diagram 2-8

segments of early practice sessions should be set aside to drill on turning this particular error into a gain.

The I-back's counter jab step is both for timing and the possible holding influence it might have on the linebackers to the inside. An important coaching point here is to have the ball carrier keep his head and eyes to the hole as he makes his jab so that as he takes his "Slant" course to the hole, he can see the blocking develop right from the snap. If the play is run from a halfback set, the back opens up with his right foot, in Diagram 2-7 (b), takes his step with his left, and then pushes off in a slant for the running area with his next right.

The linemen's play sheet assignments for the "Belly Slant" would read as follows:

Back-side End: Downfield

Back-side Tackle: Zone

Back-side Guard: Front-side gap, zone, back-side gap.

Center: Front-side gap, zone, back-side gap.

Front-side Guard: Kick-out the first man lined up head on to outside the end on the line.

Front-side Tackle: Crackdown on the first man from your inside shoulder.

Front-side End: Crackdown on the first man from your inside shoulder.

DRILLS FOR THE SLANT

In working the guards for the off-tackle belly blocking, one very important point is stressed in the Polypotent Offense. A good defensive football player, lined up on the offensive end's nose is not going to waltz across the line setting himself up for a clean kick-out. More than likely, he will slant down with the end as he reads crackdown, thereby making the block more difficult for the guard. See Diagram 2-9. A drill should be

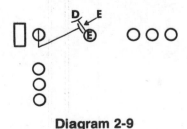

Diagram 2-9

set up simulating this actual condition so that the guard will get practice digging the man out of the hole and not by-passing him, which is a common error.

The key area of the crackdown assignment for the front-side tackle and end is recognition. Who is the first man from their inside shoulder? He could be on or off the line. Several situations are illustrated in Diagram 2-10 and these same situations can be set up as drills to school the ends and tackles for not only the "Slant", but the "Drive" which follows next.

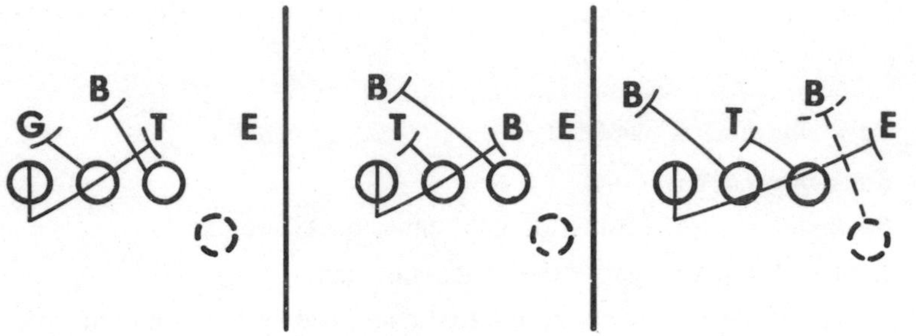

Diagram 2-10

THE POLYPOTENT BELLY DRIVE

The "Belly Drive" is the fullback off tackle. It is the first in a series of fullback-quarterback-keep—pitch-option plays with guard-out blocking. The "Drive" can be run from a number of sets as seen in Diagrams 2-11(a-d). Though it is the heart of the Belly Series, it can be blocked a number of different ways while maintaining the same backfield action. This is described in Chapter 4.

"BELLY DRIVE"

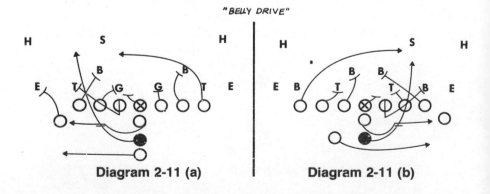

Diagram 2-11 (a)   **Diagram 2-11 (b)**

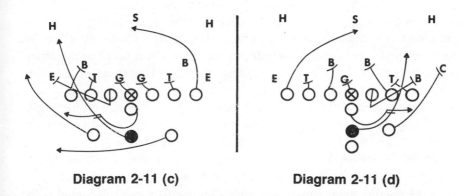

Diagram 2-11 (c)   **Diagram 2-11 (d)**

Line blocking for the Drive is a carbon copy of the Slant. The backfield mechanics are important here because they are identical for the Pitch, Keep and variations of the Drive.

The quarterback makes a three-quarter reverse pivot for the start of his move instead of the half turn he had in the Blast or the open step in the Slant. His footwork must be coordinated with that of the fullback's to make for a smooth ride and exchange. The ride portion will be especially important for the Keep and Pitch plays. Diagram 2-12 (a) gives the foot work for the ''Belly Drive—Right'' for the quarterback while Diagram 2-12 (b) illustrates the fullback's steps. The fullback is coached to hit the hole with his shoulders square to the line of scrimmage. It has the advantages of giving the ball carrier a chance to cut in or out, to protect himself from blind-side linebacker side swipes, and it positions him so that he is running to the goal line and not the side line. See Chapter 10.

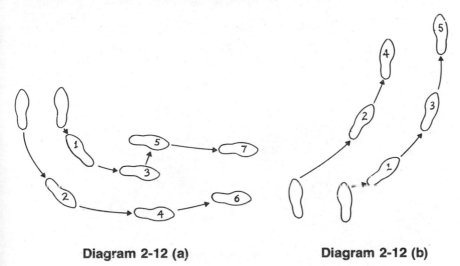

Diagram 2-12 (a)   **Diagram 2-12 (b)**

Even though this is a definite handoff for the quarterback, he should focus his eyes on the corner of the defense. This is done to get a clearer picture in his mind as to what to anticipate from the outside when the Keep or the Pitch is run. Too often, quarterback's will take the opportunity to become spectators after handing the ball off instead of planning ahead.

The wingback or lead halfback must recognize the man on the line of scrimmage who is to be kicked-out by the guard. He should know the guard's rule so that there will be no doubt in his mind as to his responsibility on the Drive. See Diagrams 2-10 and 2-11. If there is a man on the line whether it be a grounded lineman or a head-on bump-and-run linebacker, the back should leave him alone. That's the guard's meat. His read is the first linebacker (off the line) from head up the end to the outside. If there is no linebacker, then his block is downfield on the nearest man in the secondary. The back's route of coming out of the backfield can give the guard's man something to think about as he wonders whether to play a possible chop-in or kick-out. See Diagram 2-11, "T-Belly Drive Left."

THE POLYPOTENT BELLY KEEP

Though the "Belly Keep" appears to be an option type of play, it is set up with a definite block on the corner in an attempt to get outside. In short, the quarterback keeps the ball all the way after coming out of the Drive fake. See Diagram 2-13 (a) and (b).

As illustrated, the quarterback and fullback meet up for the ride over the tackle. They both use the identical footwork that was used in the

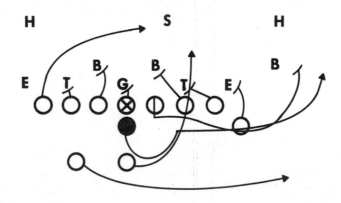

Diagram 2-13 (a)

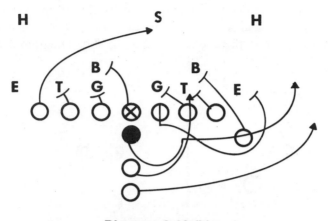

Diagram 2-13 (b)

Drive. To help the fake, the fullback should dip his outside shoulder as the ride is made. This has the effect of shielding the ball from the defensive corner and sets up the guard's block. As the quarterback rides the fullback with steps No. 4 and No. 5, (See Diagram 2-12 (a)) he lets his arms swing to the line, trying to milk the fake for every inch he can get. He doesn't pull the ball from the fullback nor does he run while faking. It's the fullback who runs from the ball as he hits the area over the tackle. The quarterback reads the corner during the fake. He watches the play of the widest man who is either on or off the line. If the outside man slants down, the quarterback knows that his guard will use a chop-in and he'll carry the ball wide. If the defender floats, the guard will kick-out and the quarterback will cut up inside.

Just as the guards were drilled to recognize the play of a defender at the area of attack for the Drive, drills are set up to work on the type of tactics which are anticipated at the corner. See Diagrams 2-14 (a) and (b).

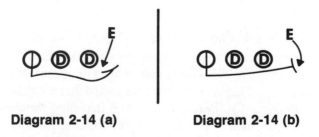

Diagram 2-14 (a)   **Diagram 2-14 (b)**

The "Lead" back can be a wing or a halfback and he looks for the second man in from the corner. As a wingback, he will crackdown. If a halfback, he uses the chop-in. Here too, drills are set up for the backs so that they can work against the types of defensive sets and maneuvers that might come up during the course of the game. See Diagram 2-15 (a) and (b).

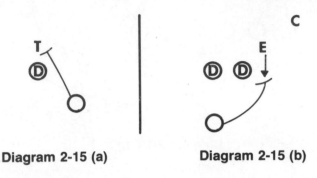

Diagram 2-15 (a)   **Diagram 2-15 (b)**

The assignments for each of the positions now begin to follow an established simplified pattern as the Belly Series expands. The play sheet reads as follows:

Back-side End: Downfield.

Back-side Tackle: Zone.

Back-side Guard: Front-side gap, zone.

Center: Front-side gap, zone, back-side gap.

Front-side Guard: Loop pull and lead. Chop-in or kick-out the widest man at the corner. Do not double-team block. If no man, lead up field.

Front-side Tackle: Crackdown on the first man from your inside shoulder.

Front-side End: Crackdown on the first man from your inside shoulder.

A very important point should be explained to the players in regard to Belly blocking specifically and angle blocking in general. They must understand that they are blocking a man who will appear in their area at the snap of the ball. That is, they must be aware that a defender can line up in one position and stunt to an other and that they shouldn't chase a defender or stand around in the running lane looking for someone to hit. If, for example, there is no man inside, the blocker should continue his angle course which will eventually bring him in contact with a linebacker or a man stunting from the inside to the outside.

THE LOOP-PULL DRILL

The chop-in block by the pulling guard is a tough block to master but, it is very effective. The loop pulling gives the guard a chance to square up and be headed for the goal line, putting him in a better position to take on the defensive man. In teaching the guards to pull and loop, they must be instructed to keep their heads and eyes looking to the corner from the very moment they take off on the snap signal. They must get depth as they work to the outside and then start to turn up. Dipping the inside shoulder will help them in making a rounded-off turn up field. In Diagram 2-16, a drill is illustrated where dummies are placed behind the line to force the guard to pull around them.

Diagram 2-16

An important point here is to be sure the officials for each game are informed of this particular type of block as well as any other "special" play which might be used. It is amazing how many flags can be thrown when a defensive man suddenly turns on impact, making the block resemble a clip. A short, impromptu rules interpretation meeting prior to the game can become a very handy "play" for a coach. Let the man wearing the stripes know you're thinking about him. It'll do him good.

THE POLYPOTENT BELLY PITCH

The corner has now been set up for the outside pitch. The "Belly Pitch" is accompanied by a "lead" blocker on the part of the front-side guard. See Diagram 2-17 (a) and (b). Any scouting tendencies of running to the wing side are eliminated by going outside away from the wing or slot as seen in Diagram 2-17 (b). In this case, the Slotback will have plenty of time to get wide and in position to receive the pitch.

Since the play is a definite pitch, a downfield blocker is needed to cover the outside defensive back. Therefore, the second defensive man in from the outside is left unblocked. He is, however, influenced or brushed by the wingback or halfback who would normally have him on the Keep.

Leaving that particular defensive man alone gives the appearance of a true option even though it is not. Against the "Monster" or rotated defense as seen in Diagram 2-17 (b), the defensive halfback would be considered as the widest man. Therefore, the defensive end would be left unblocked.

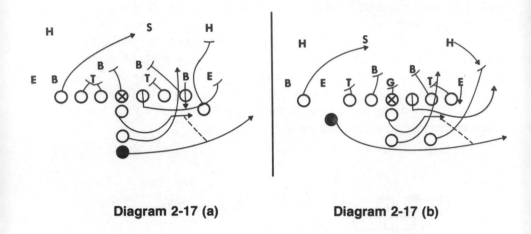

Diagram 2-17 (a)   **Diagram 2-17 (b)**

The quarterback-fullback footwork remains the same for the ride. As the quarterback comes out of the fake, he does come under control by taking five short, choppy stutter steps for balance. While he steps, he holds the ball out in front of him with both hands in a pitch position looking squarely at the unblocked defensive man. He puts the challenge to him and tempts him with the ball. The pitch is then made and the quarterback should have ample time to protect himself. A one-handed type of pitch is used so that the quarterback can use his inside arm as a protective buffer.

With the exceptions of the pitch being made and the change in assignment for the lead blocking back, the "Belly Pitch" has the same rules for the linemen as the "Belly Keep." By setting up the Keep and the Pitch as definite plays, certain pressures have been taken from the shoulders of the quarterback. However, if the talent is available, these two plays can easily be combined into the "Belly Option." At the same time, a triple-option type of play can be added.

THE POLYPOTENT BELLY TRIPLE OPTION

The Belly version of the triple-option play accompanies the Belly Slant. Though not a true Wishbone or Veer arrangement, it does have the advantage of utilizing the talents of the guard who is accustomed to making chop-in blocks at the corner. Instead of a lead back, it's a lead guard to the outside. The Belly Triple Option is illustrated in Diagram 2-18 (a) against an odd defense and in Diagram 2-18 (b) versus an even defense. If the front-side end is in tight, he will still apply the Belly concept. However, in cracking down, he must by-pass the inside defensive lineman who is being optioned for the possible handoff to the fullback. His block will usually result in a good inside seal on a linebacker. Depending on the offensive formation, the front-side end and the lead back may exchange their blocking assignments. If, for example, the Belly Triple Option is run from a Split Slot, then the slotback would crackdown and the end would block downfield on the near defensive back. Assignments for the back-side personnel remain the same for every play in the Belly Series. The center and front-side guard and tackle are blocking the same rules they would have on either the Keep or the Pitch.

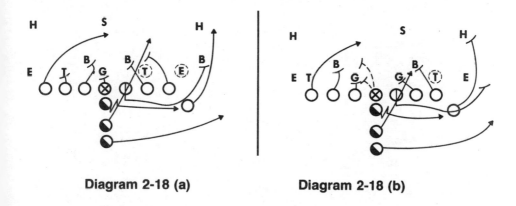

Diagram 2-18 (a)   **Diagram 2-18 (b)**

    The quarterback's moves are exactly the same as if he were running the Belly Slant. See Diagram 2-8. The read on the first option is the only new skill he must learn. This shouldn't be much of a problem if he has been schooled to focus in on the corner when running the Keep or Pitch.

    The Belly Series is the heart of this offense. It is supplemented by the trapping game, variations in blocking the off-tackle area, sweeps and a simple, but effective, set of play action and drop back passes which make for a Polypotent Offense.

CHAPTER 3

The Polypotent "Crack-Crack-Kick" Trap

THE POLYPOTENT INTERIOR TRAP

Traps are almost as old as football. In some form or another they appear in nearly every playbook, accompanied by myriad rules and theories that give just about every lineman the opportunity to trap. Sometimes, the multitude of assignments can discourage a coach from installing traps. The trapping game must, obviously, stress simplicity, and that is the purpose of the "Crack-Crack-Kick" rule in the descriptive offensive setup. It enables you to employ a simple, one-rule trapping game that minimizes line assignments while maximizing backfield sets and play action.

ADVANTAGES OF "CRACK-CRACK-KICK"

This type of interior trap blocking offers you the following benefits:

1. The elimination of any double-team block on the line of scrimmage thus freeing up an offensive blocker to be used elsewhere at the area being attacked.
2. Simplicity of rules for the center and guards.
3. Creation of good blocking angles.
4. It enables the ball carrier to get into and by the secondary before they can react.

POLYPOTENT INTERIOR BLOCKING RULES

"Trap" as set up in the descriptive terminology in Chapter 1 means that the back-side guard will pull across and kick-out block on the first defensive lineman from the center's front-side gap to head up the tackle. Ideally, on a kick-out to the right side, for example, the trapping guard will use his right shoulder and drive his man out. The center uses a crackdown block on the first man from his back-side gap to "on" the back-side guard who is on or off the line. The front-side guard uses a crackdown on the first man head on the center. If there is no man on the center, then he blocks the first linebacker to the back side. In short, "Crack-Crack-Kick."

Diagrams 3-1 through 3-6 illustrate how this rule is applied on a trap to the right vs. six of the more common defenses. The play call, backfield sets, and play action will be added in other diagrams.

The front-side guard has a "gap" rule which must be followed without exception. He should never block anyone in the center's front-side gap on the line of scrimmage. He should by-pass this man and go for

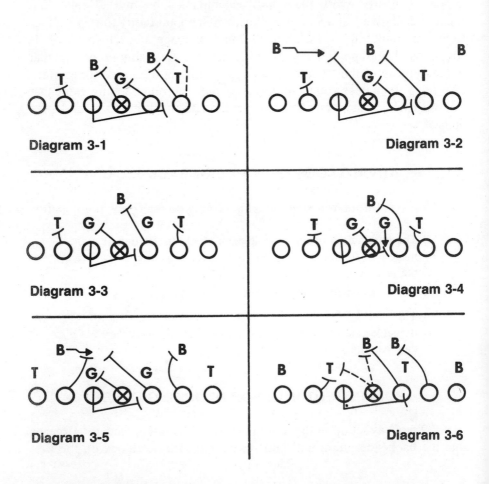

Diagram 3-1

Diagram 3-2

Diagram 3-3

Diagram 3-4

Diagram 3-5

Diagram 3-6

the linebacker as shown in Diagram 3-4. When a stunt results in a gap-rule block as shown in Diagrams 3-8 and 3-9, the guard has to veer off or scrape by to get to the linebacker.

The interior trap hits quickly and the front-side tackle must keep his eyes wide open. He'll usually be called upon to pick up the nearest linebacker inside and either shield him from the play or drive him by the hole as shown in Diagrams 3-5 and 3-6. He must determine the quickest course to take to the linebacker. As shown in Diagram 3-1, he can try to split his man and go inside or, if the man goes into the seam, he can go around. In Diagrams 3-4 and 3-9 he must "scramble" or use a "shut-off" to get in front of the tackle to shield him off from sliding into the play.

The back-side tackle must block the first man from his inside gap to his outside who is on or off the line. There are times when his man will be lined up outside and this will enable him to brush by and release down-field because of the quick development of the play. Diagrams 3-6 and 3-9 show how he'll be forced to "closedown" or "shut-off" to prevent the defensive tackle from penetrating into the backfield. He may also get help from the center in these same two illustrated situations in Diagrams 3-6 and 3-9.

LINE SPLITS AND PICKING UP STUNTS

Open it up at the area of attack and invite the defense to come. Let them stunt and fire. Encourage them to shoot. Once a blitzing defender commits himself and flies across the line, there's no way he can play off a trap block. He's easy prey and the guard will savor the opportunity to get a clean broadside instead of having to dig people out of the hole. Stunts are not a problem as long as the blockers remember that they are making contact with a defender who will appear in their area once the ball has been centered. Diagrams 3-7 through 3-10 present some inside stunts that can be worked on in small unit drills in practice. Note how the gap rule applies to the guards in Diagrams 3-8 and 3-9.

Though the rules which have been explained might appear lengthy at first, they are quite easy to summarize. You can adopt the "Crack-Crack-Kick" without any difficulty by converting it into your terms, for your playbooks, and for the benefit of your players and program. A sample play sheet for the interior trap would read as follows:

Back-side End: Downfield.

Backside Tackle: Inside gap, on, downfield.

Backside Guard: Kick-out the first man on the line from the center's front-side gap out.

Center: Crackdown on the first man from your back-side gap on or off the line.

Front-side Guard: Crackdown from head on the center to backside on to off the line. Gap rule.

Front-side Tackle: First linebacker inside to outside. Gap rule.

Front-side End: Downfield.

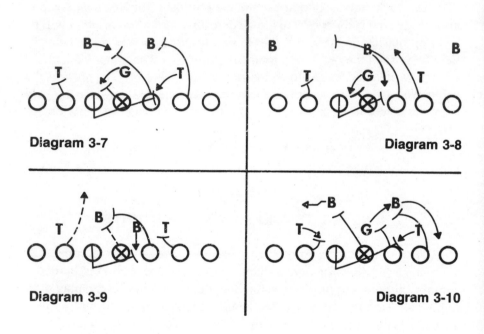

Diagram 3-7

Diagram 3-8

Diagram 3-9

Diagram 3-10

POLYPOTENT TRAPS: SPEED, BUCK, SCISSORS, DRAW, AND CROSS BUCK

The trap plays are called, using descriptive terms and are shown against both even and odd sets. When the word "trap" is mentioned in the huddle the interior linemen know its specific meaning. The backs derive their own assignments from other words as well as "trap." Diagrams 3-11 through 3-17 illustrate the various trap plays with their backfield actions.

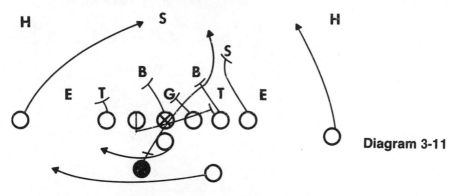

PRO-RIGHT-SPEED TRAP RIGHT

Diagram 3-11

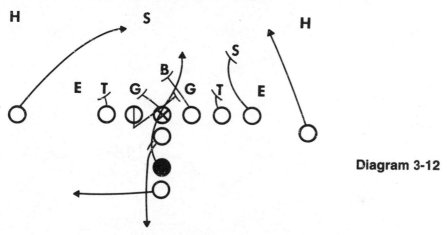

I-PRO RIGHT-BUCK TRAP RIGHT

Diagram 3-12

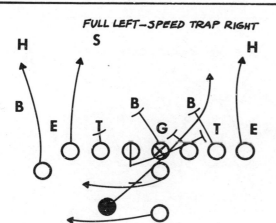

FULL LEFT-SPEED TRAP RIGHT

Diagram 3-13

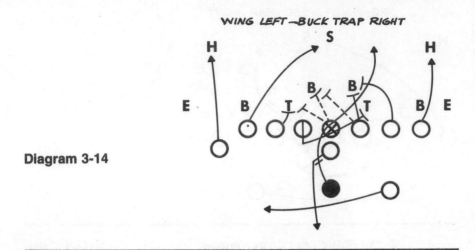

Diagram 3-14

WING LEFT—BUCK TRAP RIGHT

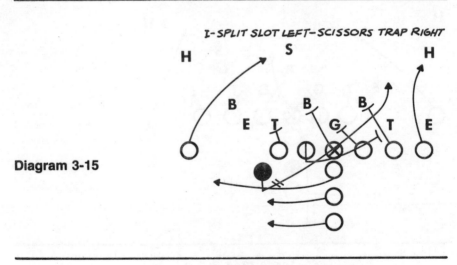

Diagram 3-15

I-SPLIT SLOT LEFT—SCISSORS TRAP RIGHT

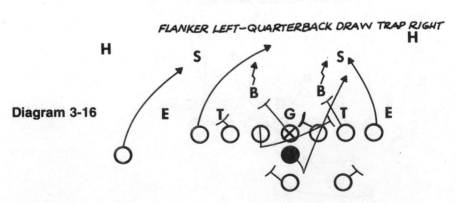

Diagram 3-16

FLANKER LEFT—QUARTERBACK DRAW TRAP RIGHT

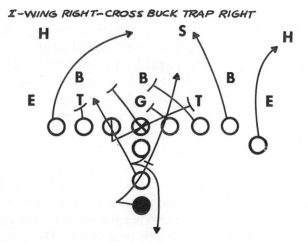

I-WING RIGHT-CROSS BUCK TRAP RIGHT

Diagram 3-17

Strategy in using the interior traps most often looks to the play of the linebacker to the front side. He represents the one defender who must be handled in order for the trap to go. If play action or a backfield set can make this man react into taking a step or even leaning in the right direction, the front-side tackle should be able to drive him by the hole with a crackdown or shield him from the running lane.

Action away in Diagram 3-11 by the quarterback and halfback presents an example of the linebacker moving out to pursue. "Pro Right—Speed Trap Right" is the play call in the huddle. On any "Speed Trap," the ball carrier must cheat up and in from his normal halfback alignment in order to hit the hole as quickly as possible and cut off the trapping guard's tail. The "Speed Trap" to the right side is also illustrated from a "Full Left" formation call in Diagram 3-13. Here it is hoped that a power set can get the linebacker to inch over to favor backfield strength.

"I-Pro Right—Buck Trap Right" is illustrated in Diagram 3-12 and shows the fullback trap with the I-Back swinging out and the quarterback dropping back to fake a pass after the handoff. Diagram 3-14 shows how the Fullback-Buck-Trap sweep action might also lure the linebacker off balance or out of position. The play is simply called: "Wing Left—Buck Trap Right."

Diagram 3-15 shows the "Scissors Trap Right" from the I-Split Slot Left formation. Here the combined motion of three backs going one way can possibly get the linebackers moving as the slot back receives the ball on an inside handoff. The slot back on this play should deepen up and favor the inside instead of taking his normal alignment of one yard out and one yard back. This gives him a better field of vision of the area he is running to, gets him there faster, and gives him a better angle.

When the backs show pass block, as in Diagram 3-16, the "Quarterback Draw Trap" might exploit any linebackers who start retreating to their zones. This is illustrated from a "Flanker Left" formation but can be run from any backfield set. The important thing is for the backs to pop up into their pass-blocking stance.

Diagram 3-17 illustrates the "Cross Buck Trap Right" from the I-Wing Right formation. Though not a true cross-buck trap from the purist standpoint, it is the I-formation version and there is a "crossing" action in the backfield. This play also has the added benefit of a fill block from the fullback to prevent back-side penetration. The counter-step action from the I-Back is identical to the Slant play which was discussed in Chapter 2 on the Belly Series.

DRILLS FOR THE POLYPOTENT
TRAPPING GAME

In drilling the guards, set up the three possible locations in which the trapper might find his target. This drill is shown in Diagram 3-18. Position No. 1 shows the defender playing "soft" and the Guard is forced to dig him out. Position No. 2 has the defensive man stepping across the line and coming under control. Position No. 3 is "trap bait," the ideal situation. The players at the three positions in this drill line up with their backs to the pulling guard. Each has a hand dummy. On the snap call, the coach shouts out a number and that particular man turns to meet the blocker. The guard must adjust his course at full speed to carry out the proper assignment.

Diagram 3-18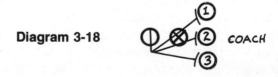

Just as in drilling for almost all plays, after the individual position work is accomplished, small group drills are next. The center and guards are set up to work on their "Crack-Crack-Kick" assignment vs. straight sets, gap, and gap-stunt situations. This is then expanded to the entire interior line for practice against such defenses as those illustrated in Diagrams 3-1 through 3-10 or the scouting report defense for the week.

An excellent drill for getting the ball carrier to read the running area and change his route at full tilt is illustrated in Diagram 3-19. It can be used for all of the backfield trap plays with minor modifications and is beneficial for the rest of your offensive running plays in that it teaches the backs to look immediately to the hole to watch the blocking develop. Diagram 3-19 is for the "Speed Trap" where three running lanes are arranged by placing four dummies on the ground. A waiting back is stationed in each of the stalls holding an air dummy. The coach points to one of the players to vacate his stall a count after the snap. This can represent a man being blocked or a stunting linebacker. The ball carriers get practice reading the play opening up tight because of a gap charge over the guard, which represents an even set, or out wider to the tackle for the odd defense.

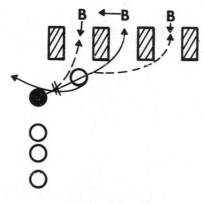

Diagram 3-19

The quarterback's footwork is one of the secrets to the success of the trapping game. It must be smooth and exact. Just as it was examined in detail for the Belly Series, the same step-by-step approach is drawn up. For each of the five traps mentioned, the quarterback must allow enough room for the guard to get through to his assignment. Diagrams 3-20 through 3-24 show the footwork and the quarterback-ball carrier exchange. Diagram 3-20 is for the "Speed Trap Right." The first step is a combination short drop step-pivot with the second step resulting in a three-quarter body turn. It is at this point that the handoff takes place. The footwork must be lightning fast since the play hits quickly.

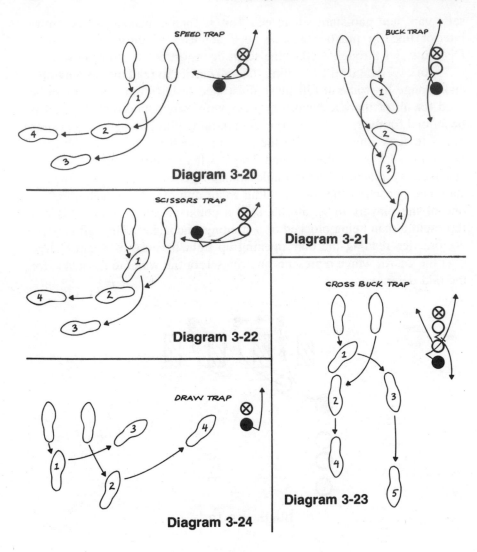

Diagram 3-20

Diagram 3-21

Diagram 3-22

Diagram 3-23

Diagram 3-24

Diagram 3-21 is the "Buck Trap Right" footwork. This involves an open handoff with the fullback firing straight up and then breaking to the right off the guard's block. The quarterback's shoulders should be perpendicular to the line of scrimmage as he makes the give to the fullback. He then drops back to fake a pass.

The "Scissors Trap Right" footwork as shown in Diagram 3-22 is similar to the "Speed Trap." The important point here is that the quarterback is moving slightly away from the line of scrimmage as he makes the inside handoff. This is done so as not to crowd the ball carrier and force him into the line of scrimmage. After handing the ball off, the quarterback should continue on with a keep fake.

Footwork for the "Cross Buck Trap Right" is plotted in Diagram 3-23. The end result here is that the pivot will position the quarterback one yard behind but with his back to the center. This creates that crucial clearance for the trapping guard to pass through. A hand fake to the filling fullback is made first and then the give to the I-Back. The quarterback must stay in place until the handoff is made and then he sprints straight back to show the pass fake.

Allowing enough room for the guard is clearly illustrated in Diagram 3-24 with the "Quarterback Draw Trap Right" as the first step is a short jab back. On the second step, he opens up and plants his foot to shove off for step No. 3 which takes him right behind the trapping guard.

Another coaching point to bring out in the discussion of quarterback mechanics is that there is a tendency for quarterbacks to wave the football around while in the process of faking or making a handoff. On all the interior traps except the "Draw," the quarterback should slide the ball into the pocket as well as look it into the pocket. On the "Draw Trap," he can bring it up to the ready throwing position before shoving off.

THE TACKLE TRAPS THE COUNTER

Teams can use the interior traps consistently throughout a game and during the course of a season without ever having to worry about holding back or being conservative. The action of the traps blends in well with other plays and they can be run from a number of different formations thereby taking away any keys or clues from the defense. They can be your most consistent long-yardage producer and pull you out of many a hole. There is a time, however, when because of smarter or physically stronger personnel that the defense might catch up to you. The trapping game should not be abandoned but, instead, moved out wider. Here is where the "Counter Trap" is added and where the tackle earns his keep. Several calls per game is the limit for most counter traps but, this type of play offers the following advantages of (1) having the potential to break a game open, (2) makes other defensive positions trap-conscious and, (3) takes away a definite linebacker key of reading the guards.

Still keeping within the theory of setting up an offense through operational definitions, the term "Counter Trap" for the linemen means that the back-side tackle will pull across the center and do the trapping on the first man from the front-side tackle's outside shoulder on out who is on the line of scrimmage. The backs know that their action will be back side with the designated ball carrier coming front side against the flow as he follows his tackle on the "Counter Trap."

SIMPLIFIED POLYPOTENT
COUNTER-TRAP BLOCKING

Execution is the key to simplicity and therefore enables the setting up of multiple formations and actions for a counter-trapping game while using but one rule. Examining the possibilities that the defense can put up against you at the off-tackle area is the first consideration in drawing up the "Counter Trap" rule. Diagrams 3-25 through 3-34 illustrate the rule and any slight variations which have to be made at the area of attack. Two critical assignment alterations are brought about by the advent of the

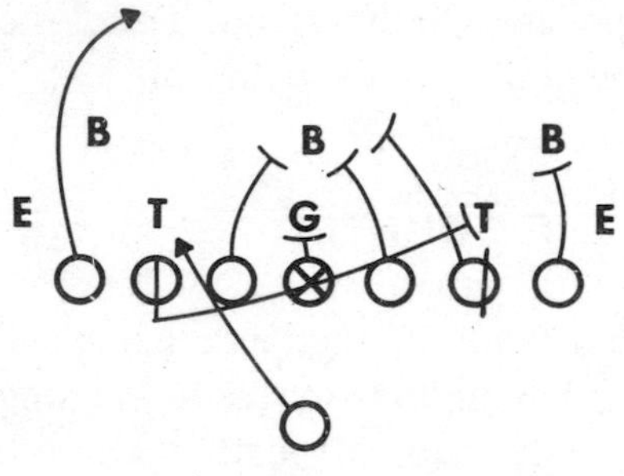

Diagram 3-25

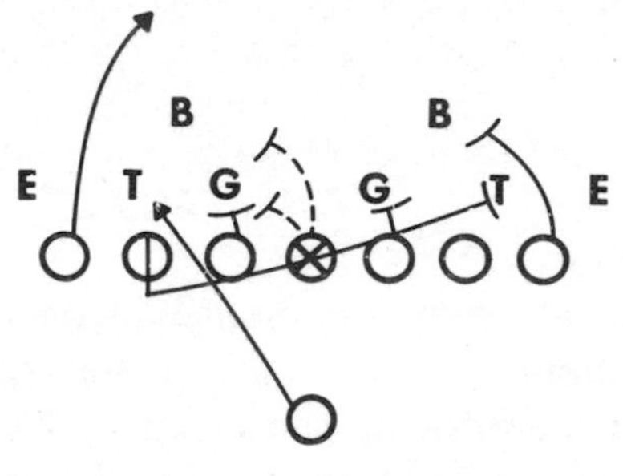

Diagram 3-26

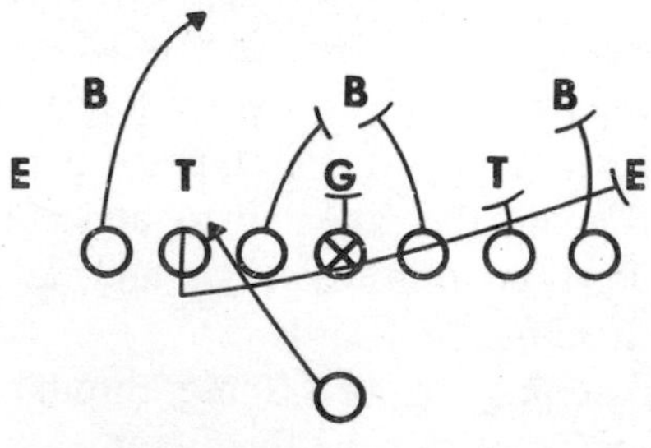

Diagram 3-27

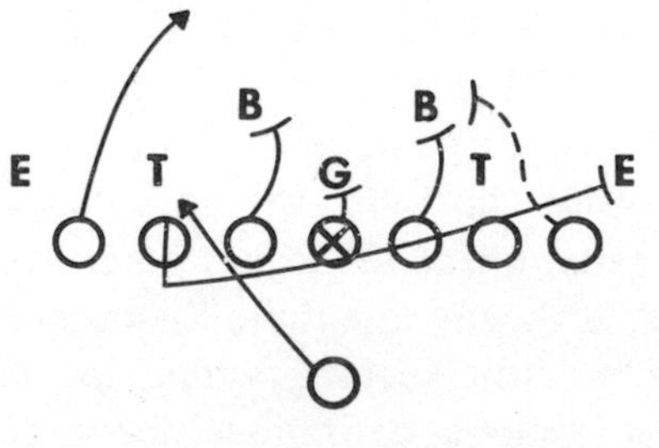

Diagram 3-28

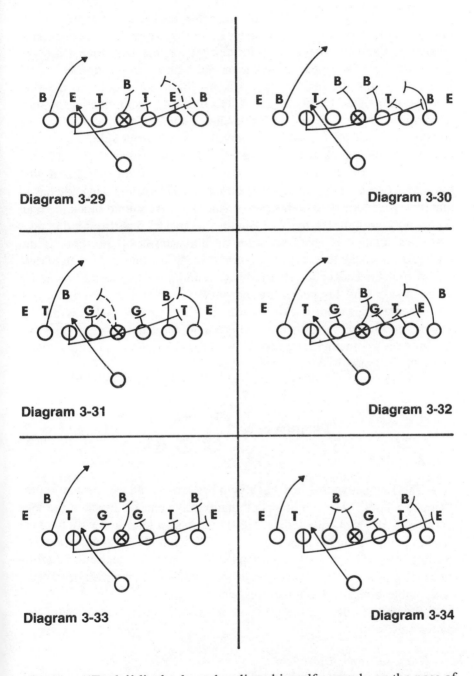

Diagram 3-29

Diagram 3-30

Diagram 3-31

Diagram 3-32

Diagram 3-33

Diagram 3-34

"Pro" or "Eagle" linebacker who aligns himself squarely on the nose of the end and camps on the line of scrimmage. By being on the line at the snap, this puts him in the category of the man to be trapped.

The blocking is now set up where the back-side end will have a downfield block on any of the counter trap calls. To repeat, the back-side tackle's assignment is to pull and kick-out on the first man from the front-side tackle's outside shoulder on out who is on the line of scrimmage. Checking the inside gap for a possible stunt should be the first consideration of the back-side guard. His blocking assignment is any man lined up on him either on or off the line. If there is no man on him, he should try to cut off the nearest linebacker to the front side. The center also has a zone block with the secondary responsibility of blocking the first man to the back side. The same is true of the front-side guard who has a zone block on the first linebacker inside. The front-side tackle has to ignore any man lined up on his outside shoulder. He should block the man on his nose or look for the first man to his inside. The front-side end's first consideration is any linebacker on him who is off the line. If the linebacker is on the line, the end should leave him alone and "watchdog" on the first linebacker to the inside. He should release to the inside by taking a step with his near foot and angle for the tail of any defensive lineman playing on the tackle's nose. If the offensive tackle is having trouble, he should crackdown and create a double-team. If not, he should continue on by, maintaining a shallow course to watchdog. This is illustrated in Diagram 3-35.

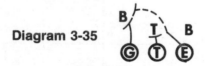

Diagram 3-35

The fullback is the only back who has a blocking assignment on the "Counter Trap." His job is a combination fake and fill block at the area vacated by the back-side tackle. He should take a lead step with his near foot and aim for the back-side guard's outside hip. This is where he starts reading. His job is to pick up any possible back-side penetration starting from the guard's outside gap. The inside-outside course which he is using will enable him to accomplish this job.

Play book rules for the linemen on the "Counter Trap" would read as follows:

Back-side End: Downfield.

Back-side Tackle: Kick-out the first man on the line from the front-side tackle's outside shoulder.

Back-side Guard: Front-side gap, zone, linebacker front side.

Center: Front-side gap, zone, back-side gap.

Front-side Guard: Zone, back-side gap, back-side linebacker.

Front-side Tackle: Head on to inside.

Front-side End: Head on off the line to inside on or off.

THE MULTIPLE-LOOK COUNTER TRAP

One set of simple rules has been examined and explained in detail. Three formations and play actions are now diagrammed but a variety of sets can be used for the "Counter Trap." See Diagrams 3-36 through 3-38

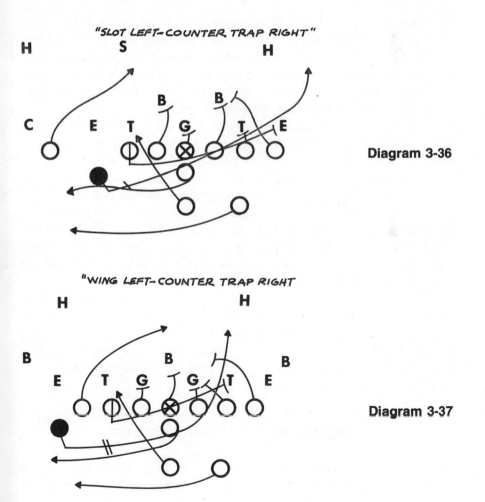

"SLOT LEFT-COUNTER TRAP RIGHT"

Diagram 3-36

"WING LEFT-COUNTER TRAP RIGHT

Diagram 3-37

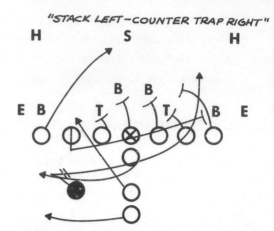

Diagram 3-38

Diagram 3-36 is the tight slot formation which uses the three-yard split between end and tackle with the slot back deepening up. He hedges back more than his normal yard to get that better view of, and angle to, the hole. His first move is a jab step with his right foot, in this case to gain even more depth. He pushes off with his right foot and heads for the hole taking an inside handoff from the quarterback.

The "Wing Left" call in Diagram 3-37 is similar. The ball carrier is tighter to his end and deeper than normal. At the snap, he drop steps and turns in one motion as he starts his course to the play area.

A power type of formation, the "Stack Left" in Diagram 3-38, shows the ball carrier taking a counter step with his left foot as the play starts. One coaching point in reference to the ball carrier's counter motion is that he should continue to look to, and keep his eyes on, the area of attack while he is making his counter move. Many backs will throw their heads into the counter fake and never regain a clear view of what is taking place between the trapping tackle and the defensive man.

So far, two trap rules have been given for the linemen. A crack-crack-kick interior trap and the tackle trapping on the counter. More than a half dozen plays have been illustrated. However, your own ingenuity is the only limitation on the number of formations and play actions that can be used to run either of the trap plays. Just two rules and the fundamentals of blocking for busting a game open.

DRILLS FOR THE COUNTER TRAP

Dummy play running for the backs without the linemen has a few benefits; timing and assignment routes can be reviewed and some of the fundamentals of carring the ball can be practiced. It's not very realistic, however, Using the Counter Trap for example, the fullback, for one, has to be drilled on his fake and fill to the back side. "Shadow boxing" only ends up killing grass. The ball carrier, among other things, has to learn to read and cut off the tackle's block. Dummy play running doesn't even come close to teaching this part of the assignment. A skeleton drill is shown in Diagram 3-39 which can be used, either live or dummy, to

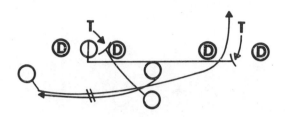

Diagram 3-39

accomplish these skills. It can also be broken down for fullback techniques and for the tackles and ball carriers. Diagram 3-22 is the reverse pivot footwork for the quarterback on the Counter Trap. He should get a bit more depth for the handoff and he should continue to run by the ball carrier after the exchange is made. The play of the front-side end and tackle can be drilled as illustrated in Diagram 3-35. Again, whether dummy or live, present several variations which these two players might face during the game.

THE "INFLUENCE" TECHNIQUE
IN TRAPPING

In recent years, the caliber of high school football played across the country has attained new levels best described as sophisticated. Individual techniques and skills, once used only by the professional or collegiate player, have filtered down to the secondary level where they are almost as fundamental to the game as blocking and tackling.

One major problem confronting the offense and the trapping game is the sealing tactic used by the defensive linemen. This was brought up in Chapter 2 in discussing what the guard could expect at the off-tackle area. The same is true inside for the trap. The seal usually results in a stalemate at the point of attack. Having been taught to slant down when he reads an "in" block by his man, the defensive lineman, more times than not, stacks up the trap for little or no gain. This is illustrated in Diagram 3-40.

The bounding, bumbling lummox charging across the line unblocked isn't around that much to be blasted into the nickle seats by the trap man. Now, strategy as well has to be used. By giving the defender several options to occupy his mind before he commits himself to react to a play, you can temporarily freeze him in place and set up the desired block. A variation in the trap block from Diagram 3-40 can be added to the basic

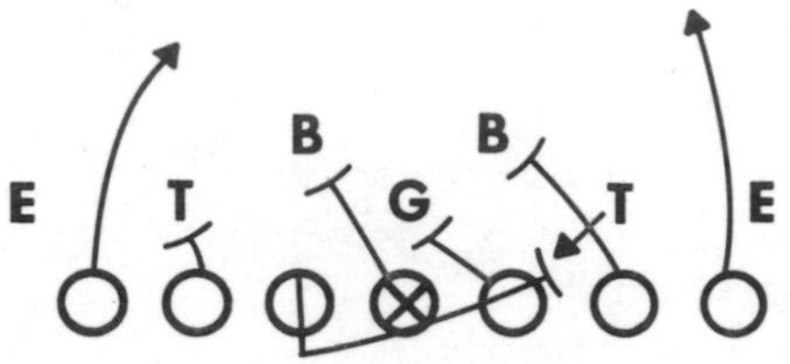

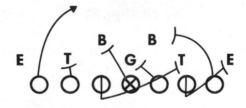

Diagram 3-40

trap rule and affect only a minimum number of assignment changes while maximizing the possibilities for more yardage. Diagram 3-41 shows that the defender can read a possible cross block or solo angle block coming from the outside. This may allow just enough time to give the trap man the advantage he needs to execute his assignment. The offensive tackle in this illustration can also take a one-count pass-blocking fake and then block out on the end. This technique has the possibility of getting the defender to look into the backfield and start to pass rush from the outside in, thereby eliminating himself from the play.

Diagram 3-41

Diagram 3-42 is another example of the influence technique used on the trap against an even defensive set. In both cases, or if it be the counter, the term "influence" can be tacked on to the blocking call in the huddle.

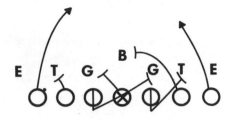

Diagram 3-42

By using the two variations in the trap blocking throughout the game, the defensive man might become conditioned to a point where he would spend more time anticipating from what angle he's going to catch the shot than playing football. There are, of course, other methods of "influencing" the defense and these will be discussed in subsequent chapters. It should, however, be pointed out that if the type of game played in a particular locale isn't conducive to this level of sophistication, then the influence techniques will have little impact on improving the output of the offense. It is very disheartening to work all week on baiting a defender and then have him stand in the hole and screw up your play.

CHAPTER 4

Exception Blocking
at the Off Tackle
in the Polypotent Offense

THE BENEFITS FROM EXCEPTIONS

Many coaches draw up simple, uncomplicated "zone" blocking rules to cover each play in their offense. While the logic behind simplicity and a clear, cut-and-dried set of assignments rates merit, the defense must also cooperate and keep their own alignments equally uncomplicated. If they don't, a portion of the offense becomes unproductive.

Various types of blocks have been examined, defined, and practiced. Here they are utilized in play calling. The theory is to run fewer plays at the point of attack but have several blocking options ready to handle the possible variations in defensive alignments.

The fullback has his "Drive" course which takes him to the off-tackle area. The quarterback has his reverse pivot footwork from the Belly Series. The linemen have their blocking combinations and calls. All of this built-in flexibility, then, makes for a more effective play off tackle.

THE POLYPOTENT "DRIVE" EXCEPTIONS

The zone blocking principle is the easiest rule for blocking the off-tackle play. Since the term, "Zone" is part of the operational terminology, it can be added to the Drive play with no problems. For example, the

"Wing Right—Zone, Drive Right" is illustrated in Diagram 4-1. Blocking is straight ahead with each man firing out at his opponent. Running to the wingback side strengthens the blocking at the area of attack. The wingback can be used for a downfield blocker or, he can "watchdog" on a linebacker to the inside who has slid off a block.

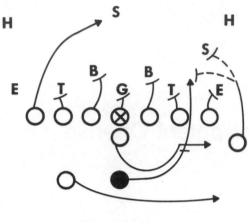

Diagram 4-1

If the Drive is desired away from the wingback, then the halfback can be added to the blocking by inserting the term "Lead" into the play call. "Zone Lead, Drive Left" is shown in Diagram 4-2. The halfback

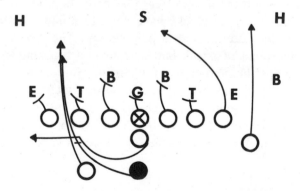

Diagram 4-2

"leads" the fullback off tackle and is inside-out conscious as he heads into the line to block. Both zone calls for the Drive are sound and, if you have the personnel to be physical with a team, this is all you really need.

However, a smart group of interior people on the defense can create problems by varying alignments, stunting, and being quick on pursuit.

In Chapter 2, the Belly blocking concept was examined along with the "Belly Drive" play. See Diagrams 1-19 and 2-11. Some of the advantages of using the belly call are that it not only establishes good angles, but it makes it easier for the smaller man to crackdown and shield a bigger opponent from the play by scrambling after the initial contact. It is also better suited for picking up stunts as long as the blockers continue their inside course. See Diagram 4-3.

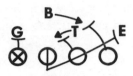

Diagram 4-3

Gaps, stacks, and gap stacks can toss the zone call up for grabs. To handle this situation, the offensive guard and tackle can go to their "Fo" blocking call. In Diagram 4-4, the "Fo, Drive Right" is illustrated to the wingback side and, in Diagram 4-5, the Lead back is used again for more muscle in a "Fo Lead, Drive" play. If the guard-tackle fold can't do the job, then perhaps the tackle-end fold combination, i.e. "Fin," will work.

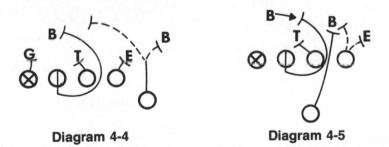

Diagram 4-4   **Diagram 4-5**

The "Fin" is especially good in handling the 4-4 linebackers. Diagram 4-6 is the "Fin Drive" play and Diagram 4-7 is the "Fin Lead Drive" against the 4-4 defense where the Lead back is given a specific assignment to zero in on the defensive tackle and give his guard a helping hand. The backs enjoy this block because they know that the first couple of times the bigger defensive tackles won't be anticipating an outside-in shot from a pesty back.

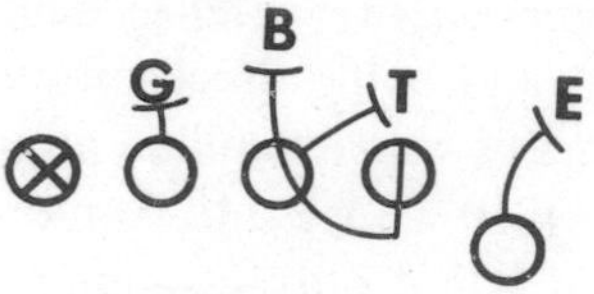

Diagram 4-6 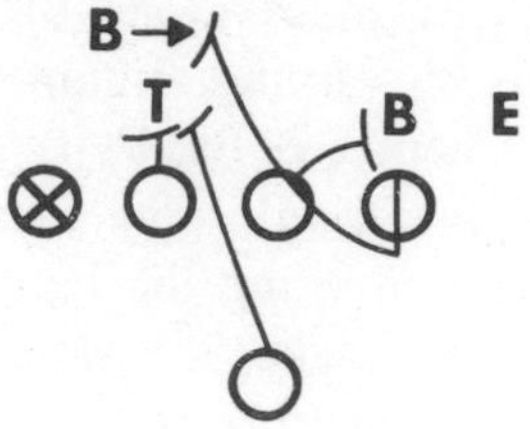   **Diagram 4-7**

Cross blocking is nothing new. When the defense complicates matters by playing shoulders or gaps, it leaves many teams with only the wedge alternative. The "X" call can create a better running lane. The wingback in Diagram 4-8 uses a "watchdog" on the inside linebacker. If the defensive End is playing wide enough, as in Diagram 4-9, a lead blocker out of the backfield can be used to mop up the linebacker. The important thing to remember in coaching the blocking back is to show him where that linebacker will try to get on his pursuit and where he is coming from. As for the end and tackle, it's a crackdown and kick-out combination with the end going first. The calls: "X, Drive" and "X Lead, Drive".

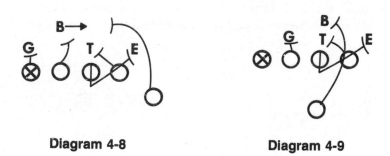

Diagram 4-8   **Diagram 4-9**

The double-team block is as old as the game itself. Since the backs have been taught to block, especially kick-out, they team up with the tackle and end for another method of opening up the off tackle. The "Power" is illustrated in Diagram 4-10. Unlike the old post-lead block, the tackle tries to take thé man on him by himself. The end has a crackdown assignment which could result in the double-team, thereby creating a solid inside wall of the running lane. If the tackle is doing the job on his man, then it is more advantageous for the end to slide by and shield off the linebacker coming from the inside in pursuit. This was examined on two occasions in Diagrams 1-17 and 3-35. The play is called "Power, Drive."

The blocking alternatives illustrated so far can be run successfully from any number of formations. They are not complicated and require only half as much time to teach as trying to funnel six different plays at one point of attack with straight-on blocking.

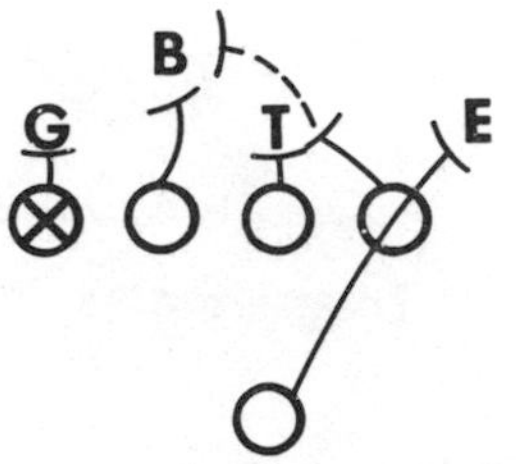

Diagram 4-10

THE POLYPOTENT I-BACK
"ROLL" EXCEPTIONS

The "Drive" was predicated on the ball carrying ability of the fullback. However, the I-Back might be the most productive runner and the fullback the better blocker.

With the Belly Series, the I-back was used to hit the off-tackle area on the Belly Slant. The backfield action and timing are too important to the Belly Series to tamper with them to fit into the "exceptions," Therefore, if the I-Back,-Fullback running—blocking talent combination is available, the Roll is installed to put more versatility into the off-tackle blocking exceptions.

A lead block by the fullback is the basis for the Roll. He takes the I-Back off tackle as the linemen execute one of four blocking patterns which have already been discussed.

The "Zone Lead, Roll Right" is illustrated in Diagram 4-11. There is zone blocking to the front side with a lead block by the Fullback. The Roll action is provided by the quarterback-Fullback-I-Back backfield operation with the quarterback opening up instead of using the reverse pivot. In Diagram 2-12 (b), the footwork of the fullback was illustrated for the Belly Drive. The I-Back takes the same steps, except he starts from a two-point stance and his feet are not staggered. Instead of rounding out his course to the off tackle, the fullback now angles directly over the offensive tackle to lead block on the Roll.

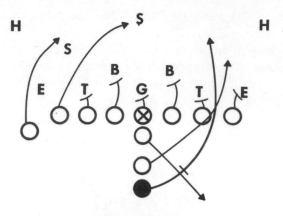

Diagram 4-11

The Quarterback's footwork is drawn up in Diagram 4-12 for the Roll. He will also use this short type of sprint-out action for certain pass plays which come off the Roll action.

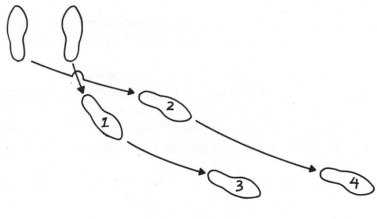

Diagram 4-12

Cross blocking has been looked at as one of the exceptions. With the fullback's blocking ability added, the "X-Lead, Roll" is another method which can be used to move the football. This play is illustrated in Diagram 4-13 from an "I-Pro Right" formation.

The "I-Slot Left, Power, Roll Right" is drawn up in Diagram 4-14. Though Diagram 1-17 shows the Halfback kicking-out, the fullback uses this technique and the front-side linemen carry out the blocking rules used

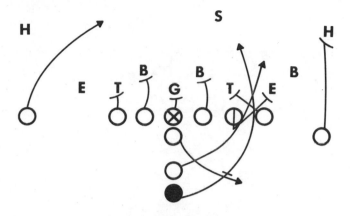

Diagram 4-13

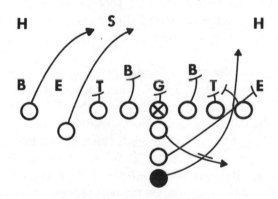

Diagram 4-14

in the "power" theory. In Chapter 2, the complete Belly Series was explained. The term "Belly" pertained both to the line blocking and the backfield action. But belly blocking is not restricted to the Belly Series. It is yet another means of trying to get the ball carrier through the line. In short, it's the line's blocking call. "Roll" is the way the backfield will function. By inserting "lead" and the fullback escorts the I-Back. Diagram 4-15 is the "I-Wing Left, Belly Lead, Roll Right." Back in Diagram 1-19, is a presentation of the belly blocking theory and in Chapter 2 the linemen's play sheet assignments for the "Belly Slant" would apply for this play.

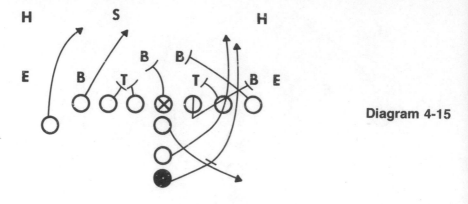

Diagram 4-15

CALLING THE EXCEPTIONS

The Drive and Roll are sound football plays designed for short yardage. One or the other is used in almost every offense and is called by various numbers or names. These two plays can be made even better by using exception blocking.

Attaching the blocking calls can be done in one of several ways. First, send it in from the sideline. This method is advantageous if the defense is reading and playing fairly straight. The quarterback can be used to make the calls. He is in a good position to recognize the defense and select the best way to pick it apart. Ideally, the linemen should call their own shots prior to the snap. They are accustomed to working together as a unit. Respect and confidence have been built up in one another's ability. And, they can be the best judge as to how to handle the man across from them. If they can mentally handle it, a great amount of pride and moral can be developed by delegating this authority and responsibility to the line. Too often, the linemen are told to keep their mouths shut, listen to the quarterback and knock somebody down. They know their blocking combinations, so let them put their skills to good use. This is also a great motivating factor in learning play assignments.

DRILLS FOR EXCEPTIONS

The front-side portion of the diagrams given so far are also illustrations of the half line work that is needed to perfect the exception calls. If the linemen are picking their blocks, false calls must also be used to the back side.

Since the backs must know how to block, their various skills have to be worked on and they must have an understanding of the "exceptions." In teaching the backs to block, it is sometimes a good idea to have them square off against the front-line defensive ends, tackles or linebackers. After all, on game day they aren't going up against the "Little Sisters of the Poor." This is especially important during the early part of the season when you're in the process of sorting through the players to come up with 11 competitors. Once the conference or league race is underway, then keep your backs healthy by going against the fourth-and fifth-team dummy holders. But give those pine riders a chance to lead, kick-out, and watchdog. They have to learn, too, and their interest has to be kept up until they can have their year. Diagrams 4-16 through 18 are a few backfield blocking drills for the "exceptions." As seen in Diagram 4-16, the back works on his lead block, with the tackle and end executing the "X" block. The back should be instructed to read from the inside-out as he goes through the cross block. More times than not, the linebacker will come from the inside, but move him around so that each back will get the idea of looking both ways as he fires through the hole.

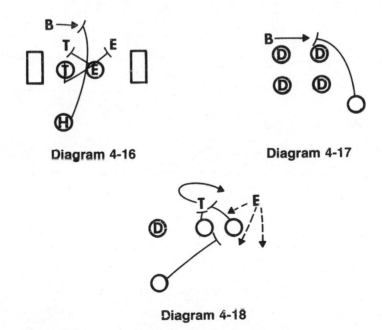

Diagram 4-16   **Diagram 4-17**

Diagram 4-18

The drill for watchdog blocking is in Diagram 4-17. Double rows of stand-up dummies are used to represent the area occupied by both the offensive and defensive linemen. In order for the watchdog block to be effective, the back must take a shallow course, almost scraping the tails of the defense as he uses a crackdown on the linebacker trying to pin him into the line.

Whether the kick-out on the "power" comes from the halfback or fullback, the course must be from the inside-out and the read must be from the inside-out. In Diagram 4-18, the fullback makes the kick-out but the drill is also illustrated with the defensive end carrying out three different charges. The back must anticipate these when he's heading in to make the kick-out. The drill also shows the defensive tackle spinning out of the double-team block portion of the "power." This is a common tactic, so the crackdown people should know how to handle the spin.

If the terms are learned in the beginning; if the individual blocks are mastered in the early stages of the season: if the communication in play calling is understood; then flexibility is available for the offense. It seems foolish to spend hours of valuable practice time on backfield coordination for a number of different plays to be run off tackle only to have it all go down the drain because the X's are not doing what the conventional O's expect.

CHAPTER **5**

The Polypotent Sweep:
One Rule—Multi-Action

THE POLYPOTENT SWEEP THEORY

So far, getting the ball outside was accomplished by using either the Keep-Pitch or Option portions of the Belly Series. Another alternative method is the "Sweep." It is a reliable means of skirting the perimeter because it reduces some of the risks which are attached to flipping the ball on the Option.

The rationale behind the "Sweep" used here is based on theory of attack. Whether it's the Mongol hordes or a modern army on the assault, leading the way is a thundering herd or an armored unit. With the Sweep, it's the guards and lead backs running over a few corner personnel to clear the way for the ball carrier.

DESIGNING THE SWEEP

Drawing up a sweep play is one thing. Blocking it and making it go consistently is another story. There are and have been many types of sweeps. Many of them, effective. Others, a waste of time. The Pro-Sweep, made famous by the Lombardi-era Packers, is a fine play. Remember both guards leading Hornung? See Diagram 5-1. Most of us don't have a Hornung year after year, nor do we face a Pro defense week after week. So, we savor the memory of Thurston and Kramer leaving devastation in their path and go back to working with our young athletes.

Reach blocking is used on some sweeps. The linemen try to get outside to screen out the defenders and the ball goes wide. See Diagram 5-2. The guard to the back side pulls and all the backs run interference.

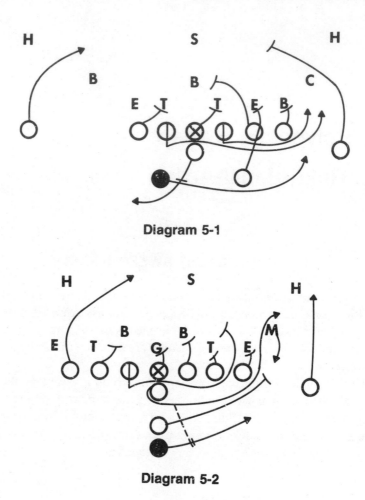

Diagram 5-1

Diagram 5-2

In the first diagram, we had the ball handed off with the quarterback carrying out a bootleg action fake. The second had the ball being pitched back. There are also sweeps where it appears that the whole line is pulling to pave the way for the ball carrier. See Diagram 5-3. The poor defensive people to the outside get the impression that half of the world population is coming their way. All a super-talented ball carrier has to do is run and get the glory.

In order for any sweep to be successful, a workable set of rules has to be set up. At this point, it's appropriate to reiterate some of the theories which comprise the offensive philosophy being explained in this book.

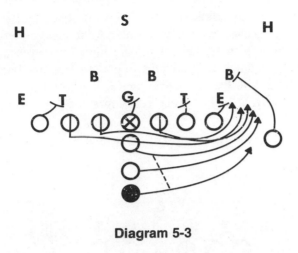

Diagram 5-3

The importance of communication and fundamentals has been stressed throughout. In Chapter 1, the "Sweep" was illustrated in Diagram 1-21 with "Sweep" meaning both guards pulling. The idea of creating an inside and outside wall for the running lane was briefly discussed and illustrated in Diagrams 1-8 (a) and (b). Developing the outside wall portion of the running lane was also examined in Diagram 1-12 (a) with the guard using a kick-out block. The advantages of the angle concept in blocking particular plays was analyzed. The assumption was also made in the Introduction that consistency is desired from average talent. These, then, are the underlying ideas used in the Sweep.

THREE SWEEPS—ONE RULE

The Sweep is designed within the framework of established terminology and uses one rule. That one rule is flexible enough to handle several problems which might face the Sweep, and simple enough for the young athletes to execute. There is but one rule for each of the linemen. The fullback and the quarterback are given the burden of having two assignments. However, there are three sweep actions which can be run. "Pitch Sweep Right" is shown in Diagram 5-4. As illustrated, there are four people out in front of the ball carrier and that's a fair size thundering herd for an escort. This is a good play and opponents have spent considerable practice time working on gimmicks to take it away. These defensive surprises usually come in one of three areas. First, the defense tries to fire all mankind through both center-guard gaps. As the guards pull, enough opposite-colored shirts come streaming into the backfield to make you wonder if you have a sieve for a line. Second, the inside linebackers start moving step-for-step in lateral pursuit the moment they see the guards pull out. Third, a team may try to unleash players from the back side in an effort to catch up with the ball carrier and bring him down from behind. This is especially true if the Sweep is being run from a halfback set.

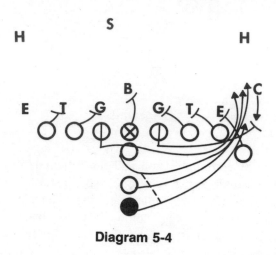

Diagram 5-4

The situations in the first two instances can be handled by going to the fullback's alternate assignment. See Diagram 5-5. He simply makes a "Buck" charge into the front-side center-guard gap almost as if he were running the "Belly Blast." This should temporarily hold the linebackers and, if there is a stunt at this point, there will be one fine collision. The center can then pick up the other gap or block "zone." "Buck Sweep," then, is the second of the three Sweeps.

Diagram 5-6 has the quarterback carrying out a bootleg fake after giving the ball on a handoff. This play is called the "Give Sweep" and it

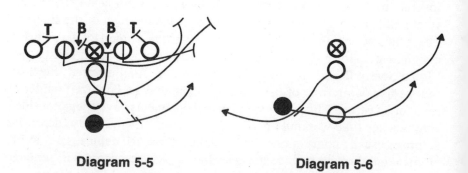

Diagram 5-5   **Diagram 5-6**

is the third type of sweep action that is run. If the buck fake were being used, the play would be called, "Buck Sweep Give." The term "bootleg" is avoided because it has a particular meaning of its own for both the quarterback and the line. It is a particular blocking assignment and backfield action pertaining to the passing game and is covered in Chapter 6. "Bootleg" was illustrated in Diagram 1-24.

THE LINEMEN'S RULES

The "Sweep" uses basic existing skills. It takes advantage of the guard's ability to pull and kick-out. The fullback's fill block is used on the Buck Sweep. Halfbacks are "lead" blocking and wingbacks are using crackdown or watchdog blocks. The entire front side of the line is doing nothing more than a slight variation of the existing off-tackle Belly rule. To the back side, there's a loop pull from the guard and shut-off blocks coming from the end and tackle.

A defensive worksheet, as illustrated in Diagram 5-7, is a helpful tool in checking the feasibility of blocking rules. Though by no means complete, it does present many of the combinations which have to be handled by the blockers. Since the Sweep can be run from either a wing or halfback set, these positions are drawn in on the worksheet with a broken line. They are important key blocks without which there would be no Sweep.

Before discussing sets and backfield actions, the individual blocking assignments are given and then summarized on a sample play sheet.

Starting from the back side of the line, the end and tackle tighten their splits down to one foot. With the back-side guard loop pulling on the play, the end and tackle must be in position to be sure to cut off any penetration. If there is one thing that is feared worse than the plague, it's those defensive people, prancing untouched across the line of scrimmage into the backfield, to break up the play before it gets started. Therefore, their job is to shut off penetration and defensive pursuit to the back side. Both players slide laterally one full man, on the snap of the ball, to carry out the "shut-off." This technique is shown in Chapter 9.

The back-side guard also takes a one-foot split and uses the loop-pull technique to lead the ball carrier up and through the running lane. He is inside-conscious all the way. As he pulls, he looks for any pursuit breaking loose from the front-side blocks.

As the center lines up, he checks both gaps for the possibility of a stunt even though his basic assignment is "zone." If too much pressure starts coming from the inside, then the Buck Sweep is called to get the fullback's help.

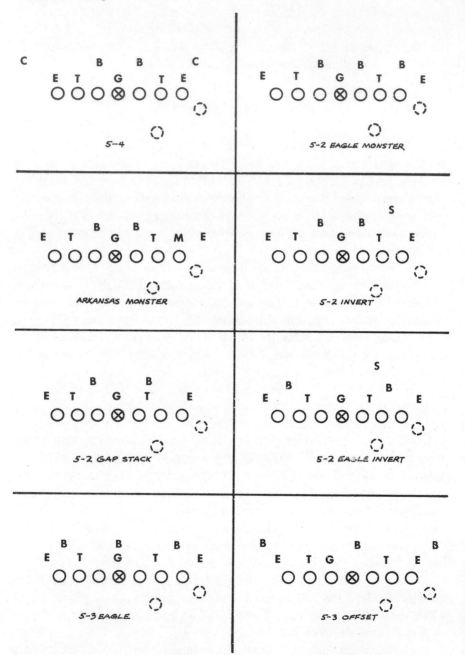

Diagram 5-7

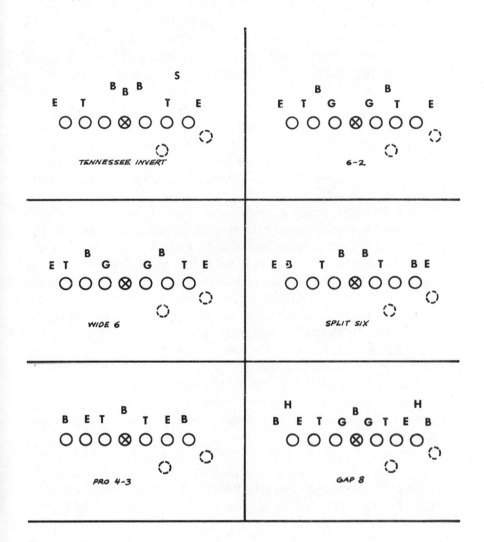

Diagram 5-7 (Continued)

The splits to the front side are one foot for the guard and two feet for the tackle. The end's split rule depends on where the defender on to outside of him has been lining up. If the defensive end is playing the outside shoulder, then the offensive end should try to waltz him out to four feet. If the defender is playing on the nose or inside shoulder and there's another defender to the outside, then the split should be cut down. The end has to recognize his own ability to make a crackdown on the first man from his inside shoulder who is on or off the line. There is always the possibility that he could split himself out of the play and take away any chance of making the crackdown. Of course, if this happens, his man has a piece of the ball carrier.

There are some variations which the front-side end has to look for when he lines up because the first man from his inside shoulder could be in a number of locations. In the case of the 4-4, the first man to his inside, for example, who would be unblocked will be the inside linebacker over the guard area. Versus a 5-2 Eagle, it might be a linebacker on or off the line who could be on his inside shoulder. There could also be a man in his inside gap. If he's faced with a tandem problem as in a 6-2 set, his man is on the line and the linebacker will be handled by the lead back.

A crackdown is also the tackle's assignment. He starts to look for the first man from his inside shoulder who is on or off the line. If the tackle finds he can't control his man with the crackdown, then he should go to the closedown. This is true, as well, for the front-side end in carrying out his block. If the defense to the front side penetrates, then the Sweep is in big trouble.

Some coaches are anti-near shoulder or crackdown blocks and their reasoning is based on the factor of control. They argue that a defensive man firing straight ahead cannot be contained and will make too much penetration. True, there will be penetration. But, not that much. First of all, you are dealing with two bodies going in two different directions and a ball which is going in a third. See Diagram 5-8. The blocker's own momentum and body position will prevent the defensive man from coming straight across and the position of his head will make it more difficult

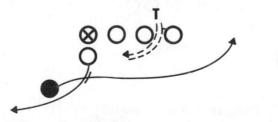

Diagram 5-8

for the defensive man to roll out of the block. Since the ball is going the opposite way, the defensive man is in no position to make any kind of a tackle.

The front-side guard is accustomed to making the kick-out block from his Belly assignments. His rule starts with his reading the first defender who appears from the end's outside shoulder. This is a real challenge for him. The man he is to block can be either on or off the line. See Diagrams 5-9 (a) and (b). The guard also knows that the trailing

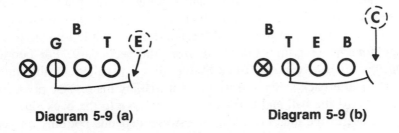

Diagram 5-9 (a)   Diagram 5-9 (b)

guard, lead back(s) and ball carrier will be reading his block before they commit to cut up or go around. A kick-out is desired so that the outside portion of the running lane wall is formed. The ball carrier and his escort can then cut up inside and start heading for the goal line. If the outside defender slants down, then the guard has to use a chop-in and the entire play goes wider. See Diagram 5-10.

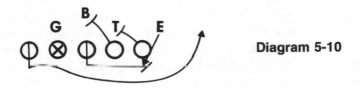

Diagram 5-10

The Sweep can be run from a number of sets. For simplicity's sake, it will be discussed from a tight-end formation only and illustrated with lead blocks coming from either the wing or halfback. Regardless of where he lines up, the lead back must know and recognize whom the front-side guard will be working against. That defensive man is left alone. The back will be blocking out on the corner or using either a crackdown or a watchdog to the inside. When he lines up, the back starts reading from the outside in to pick up his man. Because of the blocking variations to be handled, the lead backs and guards are drilled together so that they can coordinate their efforts and get accustomed to one another.

The fullback's assignment of being a lead blocker can come in one of two places. His job on leading the Sweep is to run an angle course at the front-side guard's man. His charge at the guard's assignment gives that defender plenty to think about. Not only are the guard and fullback headed in his direction, but there is a halfback or wingback whom he also has to worry about. The fullback reads the guard's block and takes the proper route along with the trailing guard and ball carrier. On the Buck Sweep, the fullback fires and fills into the front-side center-guard gap.

If the quarterback is pitching and leading on the play, he uses a reverse pivot and a dead-ball, underhand flip to get the ball to the back. He'll be cutting up with the rest of the interference while looking to the outside for any pressure coming up from the secondary. For bootleg action, the Give Sweep or "Buck Sweep Give" is called. In this situation, the quarterback starts to open up as if making his reverse pivot. He then hands off the ball and carries out a keep fake to the back side.

The use of the quarterback in the Sweep depends not only on your own personal philosophy, but also on the talent of the players. If you like to have your quarterback get his pants dirty, then let him pitch the ball and lead up through. If he's skilled with the run or run—pass, then the bootleg action is available. If he's all you've got, then protect him.

THE "SWEEP" PLAY SHEET

Keeping verbiage simple and to a minimum are the problems faced in drawing up any play sheet for the players. A basic operational vocabulary, again, is important in communicating. There are so many variations which can alter or confuse rules. These areas must be anticipated and covered on the practice field and the rule, in general, must be written up and understood by each player. For example:

SWEEP

Back-side End: Shut-off

Back-side Tackle: Shut-off

Back-side Guard: Loop pull and lead to the inside.

Center: Zone, front-side gap, back-side gap.

Front-side Guard: Kick-out or chop-in the first man on or off from the End's outside shoulder.

Front-side Tackle: Crackdown on the first man from your inside shoulder on or off the line.

Front-side End: Crackdown on the first man from your inside shoulder on or off the line.

Wingback or Halfback: The first man from outside to inside the guard's assignment.

POLYPOTENT BACKFIELD ACTION AND
SETS FOR THE PITCH SWEEP

Diagram 5-11 is a multiple illustration of the many backfield alignments which can be used for the "Pitch Sweep" or "Buck Sweep Pitch." Diagram 5-4 was but one set. At first glance, it appears that there is too little room in the running lane for all those "lead" players to squeeze through. This is, however, the desired result. The interference represents the closest legal thing to the "flying wedge" that the rules allow. Each

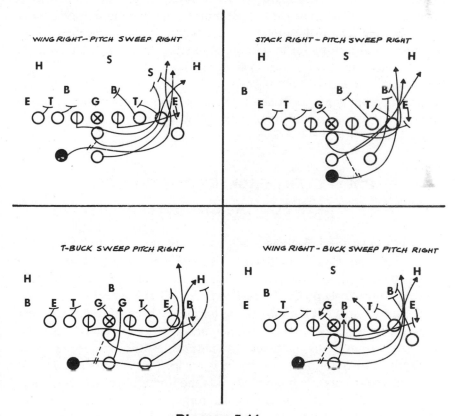

Diagram 5-11

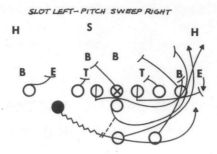

SLOT LEFT– PITCH SWEEP RIGHT

Diagram 5-11 (Continued)

man in front of the ball has a specific area to block. It's not a mass confusion type of assault. The players have been drilled on what to expect at the running lane. They know where to anticipate pressure. There is no stopping and standing around in the running lane looking for someone to block. Bodies are on the move and are being thrown. The ball carrier follows behind waiting for his chance to break out. If it doesn't come, he has his team four yards closer to the goal line.

The "Slot Left—Pitch Sweep Right in Diagram 5-11 brings the slotback in motion one count before the snap. The motion factor is easy to put into the play. It is also an effective tool for setting up and using the "Traps" and "Counters."

POLYPOTENT BACKFIELD ACTION AND
SETS FOR THE GIVE SWEEP

The use of the I-Back as a ball carrier is pretty well eliminated on any "Give" call. Either a halfback set is used or the wingback or slotback is brought in motion. Diagram 5-12 illustrates both the "Give Sweep" and the "Buck Sweep Give." To make the "Give" effective, the quarterback must carry out the fake to the backside. In making the hand-off, the quarterback slides the ball into the pocket with both hands. He is not in a hurry to run by the halfback. Instead, he lets his arms swing in the ball carrier's direction as the exchange is made. This automatically brings both hands to his outside hip which gives the impression that he is hiding the ball on a keep. As seen in both diagrams, the quarterback then continues to his left as the ball goes right. If no real effort at a fake is attempted, then the quarterback is just a wasted man accomplishing nothing. He can stand there and watch the back side of the defense pursue the play like crazy. Then he can sit on the bench and watch his replacement fake.

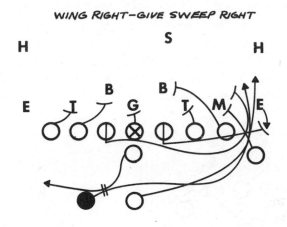

WING RIGHT–GIVE SWEEP RIGHT

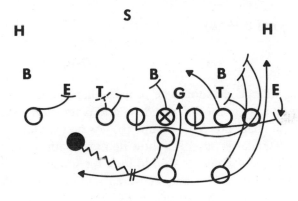

SLOT LEFT–BUCK SWEEP GIVE RIGHT

Diagram 5-12

PICKING UP STUNTS

Life at the area of attack on the Sweep is not always going to be made up of stationary X's and O's. The outside man isn't going to tip-toe across the line on every play and present himself to the guard for a clean kick-out. There will be times when the defense just won't cooperate. Earlier in the chapter, we examined several defensive tactics. In Diagram

5-13 (a) and (b) a double tandem set from a four front is illustrated showing two different stunts. The corner can become a nightmare if the players aren't prepared to handle these types of actions. The lead back, whether a wingback or halfback, as shown in both diagrams, plays an important part in picking up these stunts. If he takes the wrong man, kiss that particular Sweep good-bye. He has to think assignment, read the area, and adjust while going at full speed. His course can be predetermined, but he can't pick a man before the snap. He knows the guard will handle the widest of the two defenders and that he has the next man inside. This has to be practiced and coordinated with the front-side guard.

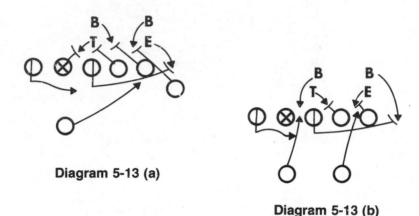

Diagram 5-13 (a)

Diagram 5-13 (b)

Stunts to the outside should be of no bother to the front-side guard. He's heading on a route for the outside and looking for his kick-out. This is shown in both Diagrams 5-13 (a) and (b). As he maintains his collision course, some defender is bound to show up in his path. Under no circumstance should he slow down or stop to look for someone to block. He is schooled to continue on through that area and curl up field if no one shows. If by rare chance the defense goofs, then it's goal-line bound and six gift points on the board.

A well-coached, alert center and the crackdown angle routes of the tackle and end should pretty well seal off the inside. Again, the idea of the shallow, continuing course is stressed. The angle routes can be as short as the inside shoulder or as long as two full men to the inside. It is important that the kids are coached to keep going and to play the game with their eyes open.

If everyone on the defense wants to pour into the backfield, then the fullback can be used with a "Buck Sweep" call. His presence should plug up any remaining holes in the dike. See Diagram 5-13 (b).

DRILLS FOR THE SWEEP

Before the Sweep can work, it has to be broken down to be taught and perfected. True, staff size and the amount of practice time are important elements in developing any play. Therefore, two complete sets of drills are outlined for both the two-man and larger coaching staffs.

If two coaches are involved, then the Sweep should be broken down where the guards and backs work in one unit and the ends, tackles, and centers in another. Some line coaches might feel miffed that their guards are working with the "ballerinas" but the continuity of the play is too important to work the line and backfield separately. And anyway, the guards should have been schooled in the basic blocks. See Diagrams 5-14 and 5-15.

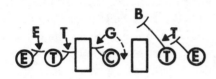

Diagram 5-14

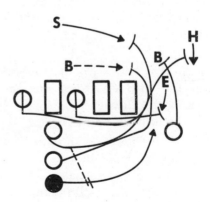

Diagram 5-15

Stunt against the small units. Off-set against them. Vary the defensive charge. Have the defense "jitterbug" and do everything possible to screw up the play. It will pay off. In Diagram 5-14, work is done on the shut-off to the back side. The center gets work on blocking gap charges and the tackle and end to the front side practice their crackdown technique against defenders both on and off the line. There are times when the wingback or halfback can be added to this group to help block certain combinations. See Diagrams 5-13 (a) and (b).

The backs and guards get to work on turning the corner and blocking their areas. Though Diagram 5-15 illustrates the kick-out and the running lane, the defender can also slant down to force a chop-in and string the play out. See Diagram 5-10.

With the advantage of an increase in staff size, drills for the Sweep can be broken down into even smaller units for more individual work and attention. As with any drill periods, the action can be either live or dummy. And, in laying out the drills, large stand-up dummies are generally used for marking positions or creating a running lane. Drills which could be used by a four-man staff, for example, are drawn up in Diagrams 5-16 through 5-19. Since the quarterback and fullback have two assignments, their alternate jobs have been drawn in with broken lines in Diagrams 5-17 and 5-18. No changes have to be made in the drills. In Diagram 5-17, for example, the quarterback can hand off the ball and carry out his bootleg fake while the ball carrier goes one-on-one in an open field situation. The next quarterback in line is on one knee in the center's spot. He is facing the quarterback who is in the drill and, with an underhand motion, whips the ball into the quarterback's hands. This not only simulates the quarterback-center exchange but, it also gives a better timing perspective to the play. Quarterbacks running practice plays or drills without some type of exchange will always start quicker than the rest of the players.

In drill No. 5-18, the fullback gets practice on his frontside gap block for the Buck Sweep. He can also work on the regular Sweep by dropping the linebacker off into a Safety position.

The drill set up in Diagram 5-19 is just one of the many defenses which the front-side tackle and end will face along with the lead back. See the Defensive Worksheet in Diagram 5-7.

The basic ground game is now complete. A good Sweep is not only important to the over-all running offense, but it really helps to set up the passing attack. Bootleg action, halfback passes, or the run-pass option all blend in well with the total offensive picture because of the Sweep.

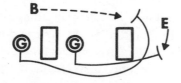

Diagram 5-16

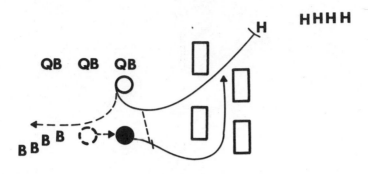

Diagram 5-17

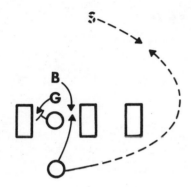

Diagram 5-18

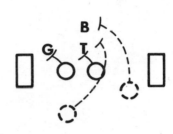

Diagram 5-19

CHAPTER **6**

The Polypotent
Passing Offense

PHILOSOPHY OF THE
POLYPOTENT PASSING GAME

There's no doubt that during the game the ball will have to go into the air. When and how often to pass are the debatable elements. These two categories are responsible for passing-game philosophies that reach ad infinitum. The basis here for throwing the football can be summed up under the headings of percentage and personnel. These two components keep the passing theory in a state of flux from year to year. The more skilled the key personnel, the more the ball goes up. Otherwise, it is thrown out of necessity or because it is felt that there is a favorable chance for a completion. This is the percentage pass. Game plan strategy and the element of surprise complete the philosophy of the passing game.

THE POLYPOTENT PASSING GAME

Several problems face the passing portion of the offense. First, the play calls have to be kept within the framework of the descriptive terminology. Second, there is the difficult skill of pass blocking to teach and pass-blocking assignments to be learned. And, finally, limited practice time cuts down on the number of patterns and routes used by the receivers. The emphasis, therefore, is placed on (a) execution of a few patterns and (b) the use of variations in pass routes brought about by either zone or man-for-man coverage.

TYPES OF PASSES

There are five different types of passes which are used by this offense. These are "Play-action," "Sprint-out," "Drop-back," "Bootlegs," and "Specials."

The running plays which have been described so far all have a corresponding pass. These "Play action" passes have a specific type of blocking and basic variable patterns. The "Sprint out" and "Drop back" passes are usually called on in two situations. The first is when everyone in the stadium knows it's going to be a pass. In general, the other time will be when the short percentage completion is needed to keep a drive going. The "Bootleg," however, is the primary pass used in this situation. The "Specials" include the "Screens" and "Draw" play as well as one type of "Special" play. The "Special" is added to the offense for each game and is designed for each opponent. The game "special" is assigned a particular term which will include the opponent's name.

POLYPOTENT PASS BLOCKING

In order for the ball to get to the target, the quarterback has to have time to set up and let loose. This, of course, is obvious. How to go about giving him that protection is something else. Pass blocking is one phase of the game where everyone gets work. There are no receiving specialists. Every player learns how to block. Those players who aren't quite up to giving their all to protect the quarterback are put into the pass-blocking drills as the passer. They soon learn what it feels like to set up behind a wall of "watch-out" blockers. That is, the protection breaks down and the blockers turn around and shout to the quarterback, "Watch-out!"

Most often, two backs are kept around to be sure that the quarterback can get the pass off. They have their own particular pass-blocking skills to master and they play a crucial part in the blocking scheme. It's not necessary to put a whole slew of people into a pattern. The average high school quarterback is lucky if he sees a secondary receiver. Don't burden him with choices. Have a "safety valve" man available and utilize the other receivers as decoys or to clear out an area.

In this offensive set-up, there are different types of blocking for each type of pass play. "Cup" blocking, "Play" blocking, and "Bootleg" blocking will be described in detail when discussing the particular type of pass play.

PASSING STRATEGY IN THE
POLYPOTENT OFFENSE

Consistency from season to season is achieved on the ground. True, there are those teams which come on the scene and throw the ball 90 percent of the time. They have great success and the fans are ecstatic. But, many of those same teams drop out of sight. Sometimes, never to be heard from again. A successful high school program, year after year, is based on running. It is complemented with the pass, which is not only a necessity, but can also be considered as an element of surprise, just plain fun, or a last ditch weapon to try and pull one out of the loss column. Whatever the reason, practice time has to be devoted to the passing game. The players must develop confidence in the passing game. They must believe that the passing game will work for them when the defense starts bringing up all 11 men to within a yard of the line of scrimmage. They must be certain that the passing game is their trump card against the defense.

Strategy, then, is simple. Dictate to the defense. Keep them off guard. Reverse the obvious. And, at all costs, run the ball down their throats.

ATTACKING DEFENSIVE PASS COVERAGES

No elaborate or intricate "passing trees" are explained or diagrammed in this section. The reason is that there aren't that many cuts or routes used. Part of the passing game theory is to be able to recognize the type of defensive coverage and know how to attack it for maximum success. That, of course, means knowing how to run the individual routes or pass patterns against that particular coverage.

The zone type of pass-defense coverage is enjoying all kinds of success on all levels of football. However, it does have some disadvantages and weak spots which can be exploited. If the defense puts up a zone coverage, then the passing game has to be adjusted to take advantage of the shortcomings of the zone coverage. The most common weakness of the zone are its seams i.e. the voided area between the pass defenders. See Diagram 6-1. As the defenders back off and spread out to protect their areas, wide seams are opened up. The pass routes then are altered to split those seams. The ball can also be thrown in front of the zone defenders. See Diagram 6-2 (a). Flat passes are excellent against the zone and flooding an area will also work. See Diagrams 6-2 (b) and (c). Whether the defense will let you "nickle-dime" them to death with the short throws is another story.

Strategy dictates that if the defense is shooting the linebackers, then there should be some type of audible system available for a quick check-off at the line of scrimmage. (See Chapter 8.) A simple call for a quick out to an end or a swing route by a back can really burn the defense if a linebacker gets caught out of position. See Diagram 6-2 (d). These are but a few basic elements which have to be common knowledge to the staff and the team if the pass is to work against the zone defense.

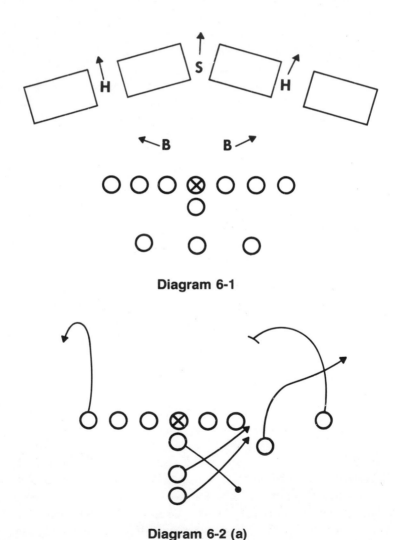

Diagram 6-1

Diagram 6-2 (a)

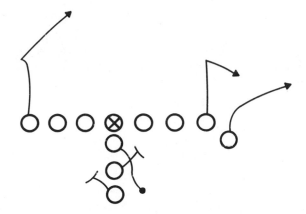

Diagram 6-2 (b)

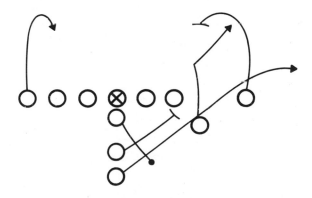

Diagram 6-2 (c)

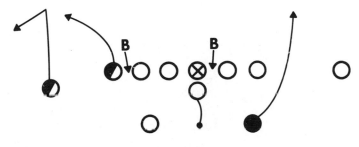

Diagram 6-2 (d)

At first glance, a team playing some type of man-for-man coverage has simplified its pass defense. To a limited extent this is true. The pass defenders key in on the eligible receivers and read pass or run. And that's exactly where the problem starts with the man-for-man defense: pass or run, Play-action passes with a fake block by a receiver who then releases into the pattern is an excellent weapon against the man-for-man coverage. Other deficiencies in this type of coverage are a match-up between an excellent receiver and an average defender and the use of crossing and legal "pick" types of patterns. These are but a few of the ways in which the offense can take advantage of the defense which uses the man-for-man coverage. Diagram 6-3 (a) illustrates the basic idea behind the man-for-man coverage and Diagram 6-3 (b) is the fake block and release play where the offense tries to get a defender to over-commit and then throw over him.

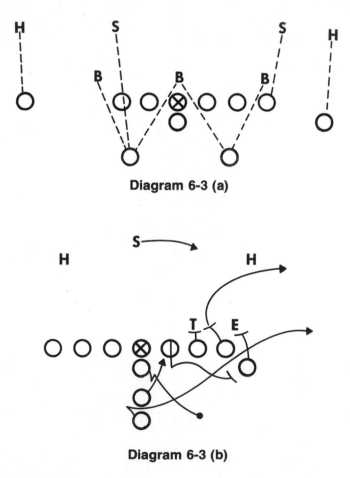

Diagram 6-3 (a)

Diagram 6-3 (b)

PASS CUTS

There are dozens of available patterns which each of the eligible receivers can run. The concern here is not with numbers. Attacking the defense effectively with a few well executed patterns is the goal of the passing game: a few flexible patterns which can be mastered by the receivers; a few flexible patterns which will become second-nature to the receivers and quarterback; a few flexible patterns to minimize mistakes. And mistakes will always occur. Two very obvious ones are first, the ball won't get to the receiver and second, if it does get there, it might be dropped. So, the routes and assignments are kept to a minimum so that the receivers can concentrate on getting open and catching the pass.

Flexible routes and variations in patterns aren't that difficult to teach or install. They can even be put in during a game. Note, in the section on ''Passing Strategy,'' there was a mention of keeping the defense off-guard. One way is through route and pattern variation. This method breaks your opponent's scouting report and is the cause of a touch of confusion and concern in front of his bench during the game.

Individual pass routes by position start with any of the wide receivers be he back or end. See Diagram 6-4 (a). The ''out'' cut in Diagram 6-4 (a) is not unique even though it is not a true square out. The logic behind it is simple enough. With the receiver driving down on the defender, he makes his cut to the sideline. Instead of staying parallel to the line of scrimmage, his course takes him on a slight angle back towards the line. This is done for two reasons. First, it widens the distance between the

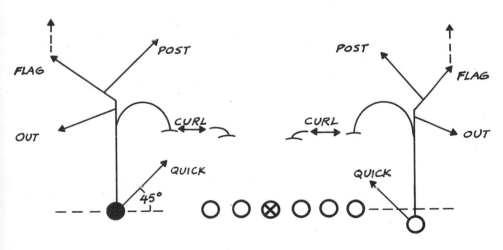

Diagram 6-4 (a)

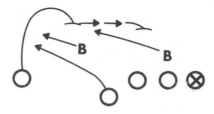

Diagram 6-4 (b)

receiver and the defender once the cut is made. This puts a greater burden on the defender and forces him to make up more ground as he reacts to the receiver. Second, in dealing with high school receivers, their natural tendency on any out cut seems to be a normal drifting downfield into the defender. This takes away any effect of making a cut. The "hook" seems to bring out the same negative elements. Once the receiver plants and turns on the "hook," instead of coming back to the line, he will back up into the defender. This mistake renders the "hook" of little value. See Diagram 6-6 for the "hook" cut.

Knowing how to run a cut properly makes adjusting to "man" or "zone" coverage that much easier. The drifting effect of the "out" and "hook" cuts might seem trivial but the pass completion percentage shoots way up once this error is corrected. And a receiver suddenly finds that his body is taking less punishment once he learns to give himself more time to catch the ball and run. He enjoys going into the locker room without his "bell being rung."

Adjusting a route against a zone defense is shown in Diagram 6-4 (b) where the "curl" is illustrated. With a normal curl, the end would find a void in the seam between linebackers. However, if the linebacker from the inside is angling out, then the end simply continues on by him into the next seam. His course is lateral and he should avoid the backward drift.

To make the "out" cut, a basketball type of pivot is used. The steps are illustrated in Diagram 6-5. The reasoning for this type of footwork is that it gets the receiver's chest around quicker, thereby presenting more of a target for the quarterback. It also makes the angle back towards the line easier to run as a cross-over step is used.

The individual routes for receivers coming out of tight alignments are illustrated in Diagram 6-6. These can be the ends, slotbacks, or wingbacks. The I-Backs, halfbacks and fullbacks have their pass cuts illustrated in Diagram 6-7. Both the tight receivers and the set backs are instructed in certain situations to extend their routes up the sideline.

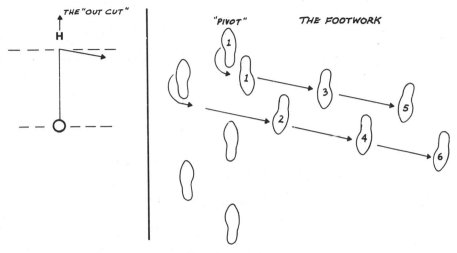

Diagram 6-5

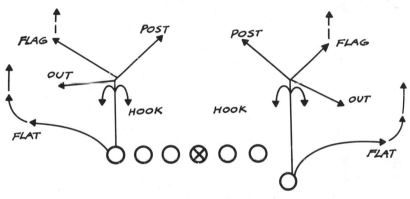

Diagram 6-6

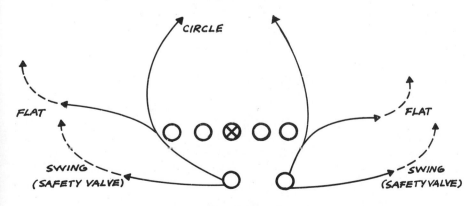

Diagram 6-7

POLYPOTENT PASS PROTECTION

The passing game uses three types of pass blocking because of the different kinds of passes thrown. A particular method of blocking blends in better with a particular type of pass play. Therefore, maximum results are achieved provided the ball is caught.

For the Drop-back passing part of the offense, pocket pass protection is in the form of "cup" blocking. The term "cup" is used because that's what it resembles. See Diagram 6-8. There are a number of systems for pocket pass protection. Here the concern centers on simplicity and the fear of defenders firing the inside gaps. Therefore, the linemen's rules are

"CUP" PROTECTION

Diagram 6-8

to read inside gap, zone, outside. If a particular lineman comes up uncovered, he can double-team block or back off and fan out to help the backs. The backs read from the outside to the inside. True, this is a very basic, general rule and analytical minds are busy picking it apart. In justifying this approach, it is one, uncomplicated; two, easy to teach; three, keeps the pass rush out of the throwing channel and, four, since the Drop-back game is limited, the inside-out blocking approach fits in well with the needs of the offense.

Line splits are no more than one foot. The blocking technique is a nose-on-numbers approach with the linemen playing the part of human buffers. They do not attack. Emphasis is on excellent balance from a wide base and keeping the defender screened out. The backs have the same type of assignment. Sometimes they end up in a physical mismatch with a much bigger defender. If this is the case, there's no way you can tell a back to butt-block a big tackle. Have the back go to a crab and try to chop the pass rusher down. If that doesn't work, have the back apologize to the quarterback, help him up, and then ask an uncovered lineman for help on the next drop-back pass.

Another view of pocket protection is shown in Diagram 6-9. The linemen block out and the backs pick up anyone filtering through the center-guard gaps. This does have the advantage of pitting linemen against linemen but, there's not much sense in giving any defensive man a chance to get up a head of steam as he comes through the gap.

Diagram 6-9

As long as the linemen remember to stay to the inside and block their area, penetration will be kept to a minimum. A couple of defensive stunts are illustrated in Diagrams 6-10 (a) and (b). These maneuvers can mess up the pass protection if the blockers decide to go and chase firing linebackers all over the field. They must stay in their areas.

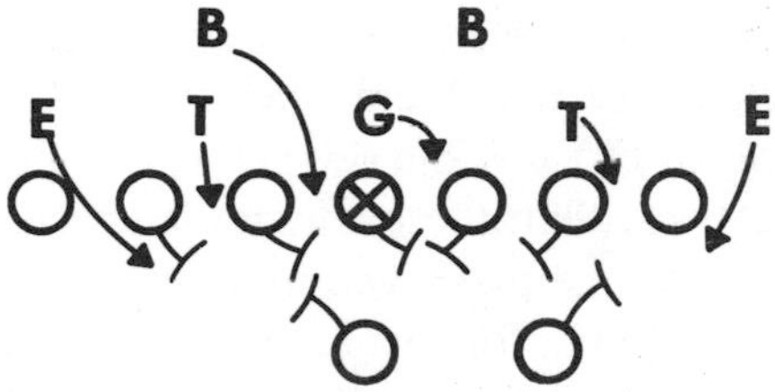

Diagram 6-10 (a)

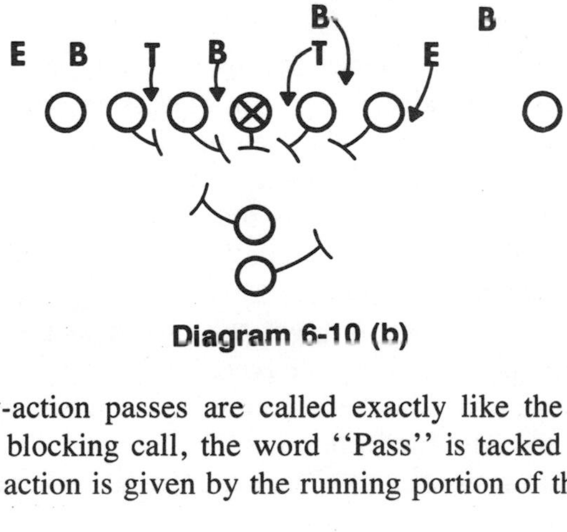

Diagram 6-10 (b)

The Play-action passes are called exactly like the running plays. Instead of the blocking call, the word "Pass" is tacked on to the play. The backfield action is given by the running portion of the play call and "pass" designates a set pattern and aggressive blocking up front. A Play-action pass call is shown in Diagram 6-11. Like the Drop-back, Play-action passes are limited plays. They are a good first-or second-

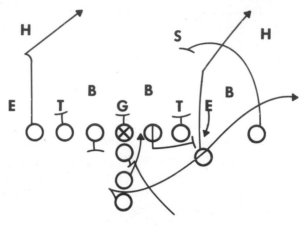

Diagram 6-11

down play in which to try and break the back-side end on a "post" pattern. If, after a series of runs, the secondary can be baited into its run pursuit by buying a fake, then the back-side end has a good chance of coming up free. To make the play even more effective, the slotback, for example, can block through before his release. Play-action passes are also excellent for working on linebackers. If the quarterback can make a good fake, there's a possibility that this will draw one of the linebackers to the faking ball carrier. Even if the linebacker isn't buying fake, if he stays frozen for a second or hesitates in his reaction, this leaves a pass zone open longer than usual.

The Sprint-out pass also uses the aggressive type of line blocking. As for the Backs, they also attack. In aggressive pass blocking, the linemen fire out and zone block the men on. They aim for the defenders outside leg and, after shoulder contact, go to a scramble. The important thing about the reach-and-scramble is the natural reflex action it brings out on the part of the defensive people being blocked. On contact, the defender's hands go down to protect himself and fight off the blocker. Once the hands are down, this gives the quarterback a clear field of vision. And, since the ball is being delivered from a spot 5-6 yards behind the line of scrimmage, the blockers scrambling at the defender's legs give the quarterback enough time to throw.

The backs are instructed to charge the line of scrimmage and try to make contact with the defender as close to the line as possible. Their assignment is to start reading from the first man outside the tackle who comes up clean. The fullback or down man in the I-tandem will get the first man outside the tackle and the halfback or I-Back will have the second man out. See Diagram 6-12. They should aim for the defender's outside and try to log him to the inside.

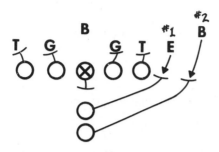

Diagram 6-12

The Sprint-out can be looked upon as nothing more than an angle drop-back pass. See Diagram 6-13. The quarterback steps out at a 45 degree angle to a spot about five to six yards deep behind his tackle. On a definite pass play, he is not to drift or float to the outside. This will put him outside of his protection and he'll end up running for his life. There are times when the sprint-out action will be used by the quarterback on a definite fake pass-and-run play. Then the blocking will be different so that it is more to his advantage.

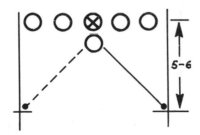

Diagram 6-13

The "Bootleg" pass is designed to get the defense moving in the opposite direction of the throw. Backfield flow in the form of a fake run is used to attract the defensive pursuit and secondary coverage. The Bootleg concept was partially defined in Chapter 1 and illustrated in Diagram

1-24. Line blocking for this type of play had the guard to the back side pulling to the front side to give the quarterback protection. The remainder of the line blocking is zone and aggressive. Bootleg also has a specific meaning for the backfield. Their response is a fake-and-fill block by the fullback for the pulling guard and some type of play-action fake to the back side by the remaining back. The entire blocking action is shown in Diagram 6-14 (a).

In Diagrams 6-14 (b) (c) and (d), the basic backfield fake actions are shown and the play call labeled for each. Diagram 6-14 (e) is an illustration of the basic three-man pattern used with the Bootleg pass. There are, of course, variations.

The Bootleg is an excellent, percentage short pass. It is also a fine goal-line play, especially if the quarterback is a runner and can utilize his talent on the run-pass option.

The "Specials" are limited. To generate spirit and build morale, a new play is added each week for that one opponent. At most, it might be used twice in one game and only for that game. The "Special" is a fun play. However, it is drawn up with every intention of taking advantage of

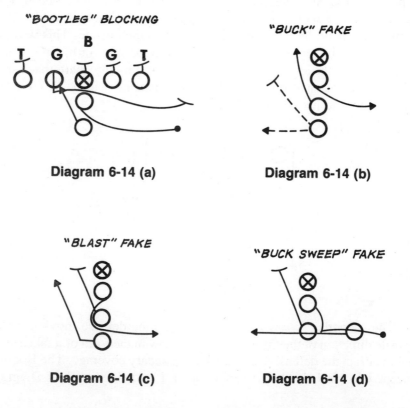

"BOOTLEG" BLOCKING

Diagram 6-14 (a)

"BUCK" FAKE

Diagram 6-14 (b)

"BLAST" FAKE

Diagram 6-14 (c)

"BUCK SWEEP" FAKE

Diagram 6-14 (d)

a defensive weakness and breaking a game open. Included with the "Specials" are two types of screen passes and a "Draw" play which uses a lead blocker.

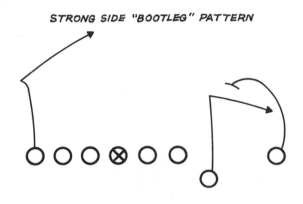

STRONG SIDE "BOOTLEG" PATTERN

Diagram 6-14 (e)

THE DROP-BACK PASSES

The various pass plays are now covered in detail starting with the Drop-back passing game. This type of pass is generally used in situations where the only alternative play call available is for a pass. And that, a long one. This arises when everyone knows you're going to throw. The defense knows you're going to throw. The spectators know you're going to throw. Even the concessionaires and the custodians who clean the women's rest room know you're going to throw. So, at this spot in the game, don't waste time with play fakes and motion. Spread the receivers, get maximum protection, and let fly.

In general, the open formations are used to get the receivers out where they can maneuver. These are the "I-Pro," "Pro," "Flanker," and "Split Slot" formations. See Diagrams 6-1 to 26. A special four-wide-receiver-out formation is also used in desperation and with the "two-minute" offense. This small aspect of the Drop-back passing game will be discussed in Chapter 8. There are also those times when strategy forces you to keep the defense honest. Then, unload a Drop-back pass on first down.

The Drop-back pass plays are called by formation, protection, and pattern, with the two-receiver side first and the single route second. For example: "Split Slot Right—Cup—Cross Right-Hook." See Diagram 6-15. The line splits are cut down to a foot and the quarterback uses a cross-over step. He tries to set up straight back about 6-7 yards deep. His one concern is never to throw the ball up for grabs in a state of panic. He knows exactly where his receivers will be because, through description and communication, he has put them in those spots. Even his "safety valve" man will always be to the single-route side. If he can't get the ball

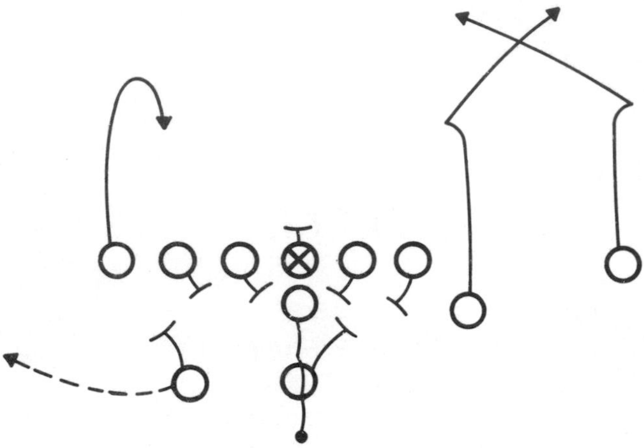

Diagram 6-15

off, then he ends up trying to protect himself. Diagram 6-16 is another example of a Drop-back pass play. It is called: "Pro Right—Cup-—Double Out Right-Post." Any number of pattern combinations can be called by description. The big advantage is that there is never a loss in translation as there is when putting a "number" into action.

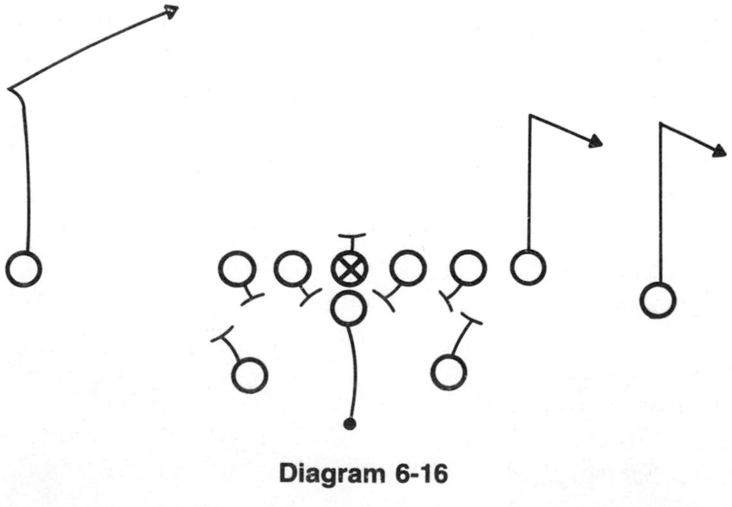

Diagram 6-16

If the tight end is kept into block, he then becomes the ''safety valve'' and the back to that side picks up the single route. This is shown in Diagram 6-17. The play is called: ''Flanker Right—Cup—Double Flag and Up Right-Circle Deep.'' When a backfield route is in the play call the end to the single-route side knows that he is to stay in and block and also become the ''safety valve.''

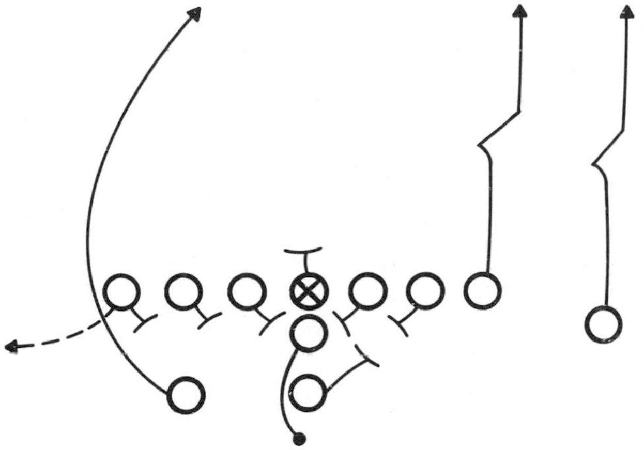

Diagram 6-17

It is not the purpose of this book to go over the training and coaching of passers and receivers. Other books on the market today cover these two phases of the game. There are, however, three small, but important, coaching tips which are passed on here and might prove to be of some help if they aren't already in use. The first point will help answer the question, ''How far do the receivers go before making their break on the cut?'' When a potential receiver comes up to the line of scrimmage the first thing he looks for are the ''sticks'' and the down marker. He can forget to wear his supporter but he'll always know down and distance. That's one of his jobs and that indicates to him in general where to make his cut. The worst sin a receiver can commit is to catch a third down pass for a five-yard gain when you need six to keep the drive alive.

The second coaching point also deals with the receivers and catching the football. Hand position and ''making a basket'' are a part of any basic instruction in coaching receivers. However, if that player can grab the ball cross-handed and hang on to it, then let him do it the way he feels most comfortable. Of course, as long as it produces results. The point which is tossed at the receivers constantly is, ''look the ball into your hands!'' Some receivers start hearing foot-steps coming up behind them the moment the ball hits them in the hands. At that point, they start to turn around and look for a tackler and drop the pass. An excellent drill to help break receivers of this bad habit and to get them to concentrate on catching the ball is illustrated in Diagram 6-18 (a). When working with the receivers on their pass cuts, station defenders downfield in the exact area of the pass route. They have air dummies and their job is to give the receiver a blind side jolt as he catches the ball. Since the defenders in the drill know the cut, they can time their impact with the ball reaching the receiver.

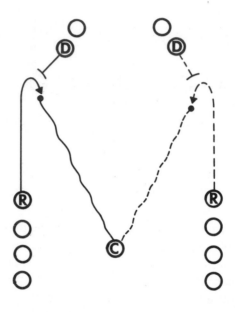

Diagram 6-18 (a)

The final coaching point which has proved of value deals with the quarterbacks after they release the ball on a pass. If a pass has been thrown in the direction of the sideline, i.e. flat, swing, out, the quarterbacks are instructed to make tracks for that sideline and yell, ''Cover!'' See Diagram 6-18 (b). By sprinting toward the sideline after the throw, the quarterback can put himself in excellent position to take away any return of a sideline interception. ''Cover'' is his own oral reminder to get moving after the throw. It's a difficult point to get across to a kid who wants to stand there and pout after one of his passes has been picked off for six points. The quarterback knows that his primary job is to concentrate on delivering the ball. But, after the release and follow-through, he must remember that he is still part of the team and that the play doesn't end until that whistle blows.

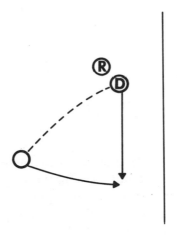

Diagram 6-18 (b)

THE SPRINT-OUT PASS PLAYS

The short Sprint-out pass used here is based on the following theory. Pass defenses are usually coached to recognize action or drop passes so that some type of rotation or coverage can be put into effect. The question is, "What distinguishes action from drop back?" If the quarterback, for example, starts out by opening up to his right and gets depth at a 45° angle, does this indicate drop-back or action coverage to the secondary? Does the secondary roll or play straight? Do they stay in a predetermined call regardless of which way the quarterback goes? Does the quarterback's action cause an invert coverage or does it pull a linebacker out of a zone? Does the end to the back side drop off or trail?

One view is that if the quarterback drops straight back it's most naturally drop back. Another side states that if the quarterback stays within his tackles, this is drop back. Once he gets outside of tackle contain, then the pass play goes into the action category. This is illustrated in Diagram 6-19.

It is hoped that the quarterback's action will get the defense moving in a certain direction. This way the offense dictates to the defense and certain patterns will be set up to our advantage.

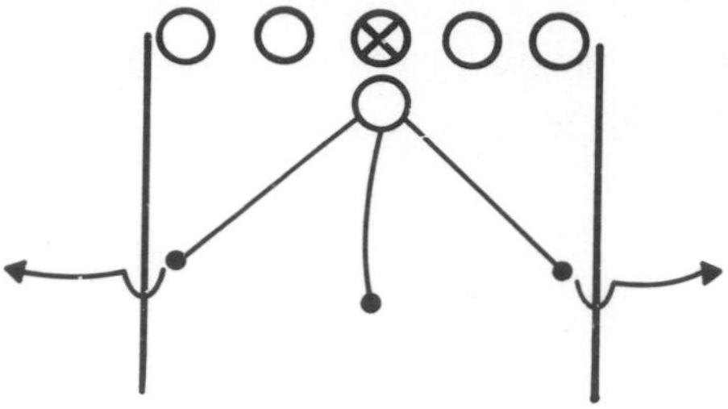

Diagram 6-19

The Sprint-out pass also uses the tight one-foot line splits. Some people might say this is a definite key for throwing. Maybe so. But, no pass rusher is going to be given a 3-4 foot split to shoot through. He'll be in the backfield faster than if he had lined up there prior to the snap of the ball. Maximum protection is a must. And, on the Sprint-out pass plays the blocking is aggressive along the line and for the backfield. See Diagram 6-12. The quarterback's Sprint-out action was shown in Diagram 6-13. By setting up at this point behind the tackle, the quarterback is possibly forcing the defense to commit itself to action or drop-back coverage. It's frustrating for the secondary to see the quarterback apparently showing action and then pull up to throw. This is especially true if the run-pass option is a part of the offense. One extra step by the quarterback, putting him outside his tackle, might force a defense into a different coverage. Better yet, part of the defense might go into drop-back and the other cover action. And still better, they might hesitate. Then it's a matter of the thrower and receiver playing catch.

From his setup position behind the tackle, the quarterback is in an excellent position for the throwback pass or "trans-continental." Once outside the tackle contain, the throwback becomes more difficult.

Diagrams 6-20 through 6-23 illustrate four Sprint-out" passes. The play call is tagged on to each of the diagrams. Unlike the Drop-back pass plays, the blocking is not called. To the blockers, Sprint-out means an aggressive blocking assignment.

Unless otherwise indicated, the single receiver to the back side will always try to split the deep middle by running a "post." Therefore, his route is not called in the huddle. The pattern to the front side reads from the outside in with the widest receiver taking the first cut called. As with the Drop back, any two-man pattern scheme can be called to attack the defense. There are specific set patterns with the Sprint-out passes. The

"Flood" call in Diagram 6-21 puts three receivers in the outside zone. "Flood" automatically means "flag" and "out" to the two normal receivers and the I-Back or halfback gives up his block for a "flat" route.

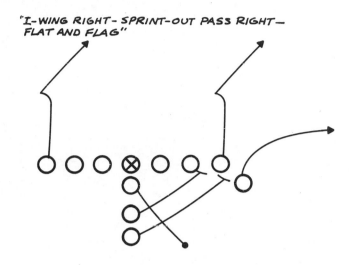

Diagram 6-20

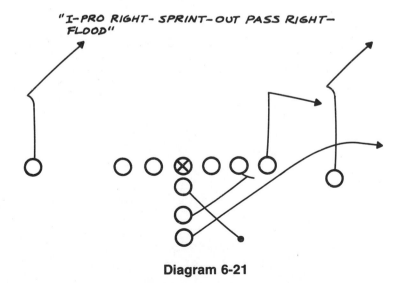

Diagram 6-21

For any "throwback" passes out of the Sprint-out, the two receivers will always run a "curl-out" combination. This is shown in Diagrams

6-22 and 6-23. The "Throwback" in Diagram 6-22 has the halfback running a "swing" up the side line. If a careless defensive back starts to vacate his zone and wander with the "post" cut, then the ball is thrown

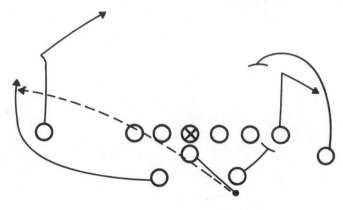

Diagram 6-22

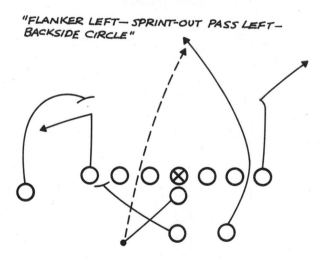

Diagram 6-23

back opposite action. It is important to find out early in the game how your opponent is playing action away. A slow linebacker and a fast halfback make for a great match-up.

The "Back-side Circle" call is the only time that the single receiver deviates from his "post" assignment. In Diagram 6-23, the "curl-out" is shown to the action side and the tight receiver runs a "flag" trying to spread out the middle. The halfback then runs a "circle" into the vacated deep middle.

The Sprint-out passes are condensed and summarized for simplicity in Chart 6-1 in the following manner:

CALL	RECEIVER'S ROUTES
"Sprint-out" (basic)	Flat and Flag front side. Back-side Post.
"Flood"	Flag and Out front side. I-Back or halfback Flat. Back-side Post.
"Throwback"	Curl and Out front side. Back-side Post and halfback Swing.
Back-side Circle	Curl and Out front side. Back-side Flag and halfback Circle.

Chart 6-1

THE PLAY-ACTION PASS PLAYS

Faking the run and then throwing the ball is a great weapon. Anywhere from seven to nine men can be temporarily frozen at the line of scrimmage if the play fake is decent. This gives the receivers that one or two extra-step advantage that they need to get open.

Protection can sometimes be a problem since this type of pass takes a bit longer to get off. Just because there's a fake, doesn't mean that the defense won't be aggressive. And, there's always someone far enough removed from the holding influence of the fake who ends up greeting the quarterback before the ball gets released. Blocking is also rough on the backs. Not only do they have the responsibility of making a good fake, but they also have to fill and pass block.

Play-action pass blocking for the line is really a conglomeration of "cup," "aggressive," and pulling linemen. When a play-action pass is called it indicates that a particular lineman to the front side will pull and protect to the back side. As for which lineman pulls, the play call will designate him. For example, the "Blast" is run over the guard's area. See Diagram 2-1. On the "Blast Pass," the guard will pull back side and pick up the first man who appears from the back-side tackle's outside hip. This is illustrated in Diagram 6-24 (a). The fullback will fill block for him. The "Drive" is an off-tackle area play. See Diagrams 2-11, 4-1 and 4-2. Therefore, the front-side tackle pulls back side as the fullback fakes and fills. See Diagram 6-24 (b). Outside protection comes from the trailing back as he starts reading the first man from the tackle's outside hip. Uncovered linemen take a fire-out step charge and then block "cup." If unattacked, they deepen up on an angle toward the passer to give him extra protection.

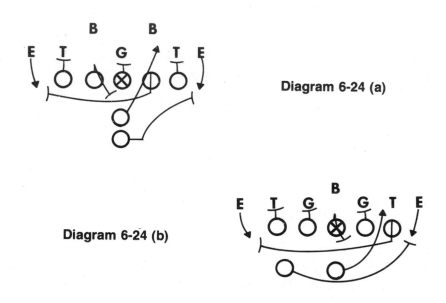

Diagram 6-24 (a)

Diagram 6-24 (b)

Four Play-action passes coming off four different play fakes are illustrated in Diagrams 6-25 through 6-28. In general, one set pattern is used. The two receivers to the front side run a "flat-curl" combination. Back side, it's a "flag-and side-line" route. The widest receiver to the front side will always run the "curl" while the second man in goes "flat."

The quarterback uses the same footwork as if he were executing the running play. After the fake, he drops straight back. This puts him in a position which is approximately the same as if he were releasing the ball for a Sprint-out.

In all Play-action pass cases, the sideline becomes the "safety valve." The quarterbacks are instructed to overthrow the receivers if they are covered. It's better to have a cheerleader catch the ball than risk an interception by trying to force it into a "crowd."

The only variation in the footwork for the quarterback comes on the "Buck Sweep Pass." See Diagrams 6-28 and 5-12. Instead of carrying out the keep fake, the quarterback rides the halfback and then follows behind to set up for the throw.

FLANKER RIGHT—DRIVE PASS RIGHT

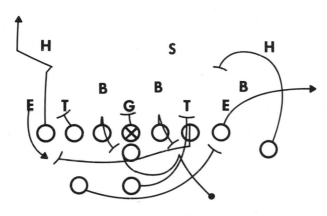

Diagram 6-25

SPLIT SLOT RIGHT—SLANT PASS RIGHT

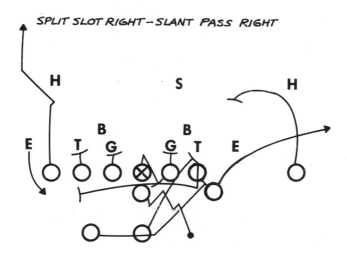

Diagram 6-26

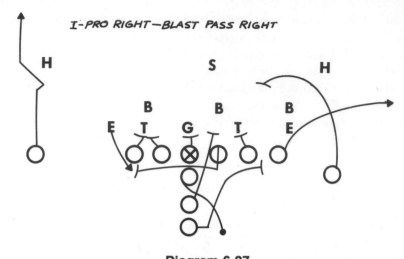

Diagram 6-27

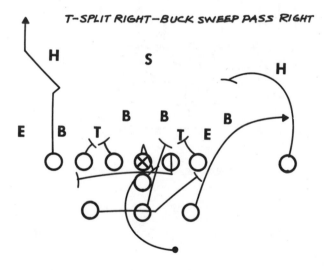

Diagram 6-28

THE BOOTLEG PASS PLAYS

The Bootleg passes could come under the Play-action category since a run fake is used to try and fool the defense. The primary difference is that the fake is back side and the quarterback is going opposite to throw or possibly make it to the outside with the help of a ''lead'' guard or by himself.

There are two general Bootleg calls. The first is where the ball will be thrown to the two-receiver side. This is illustrated in Diagram 6-29. The second type is to the single-receiver side and is illustrated in Diagram 6-30.

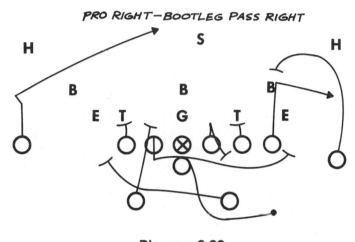

Diagram 6-29

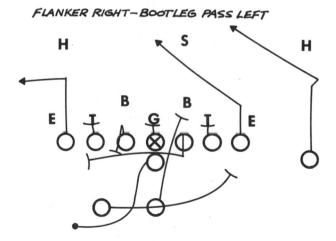

Diagram 6-30

The receivers have very simple rules to follow for their bootleg patterns. If the play is to the two-receiver side, then there is a "curl-out" combination run with the widest man curling back. The single back-side receiver runs a "long post." He does not get as deep before he makes his cut. Instead, he makes his break about three yards off the line and runs a diagonal route. On a bootleg pass to the single-receiver side, the end makes a normal ''out'' cut. The two receivers back side are both running ''post'' patterns. A normal ''post'' is used by the inside receiver. In this way, distance can be maintained between the receivers while still putting them in a practical position for a pass.

To break any possible key to the bootleg pass because of the ''Pro'' set and the ''Sweep'' fake, other play actions can also be used. This is shown in Diagram 6-31 (a) where a ''Blast'' fake is shown by the back-field. The ''Blast'' call doesn't change the blocking. A guard still pulls and a back fills.

The Bootleg is the highest percentage pass in the offense. Though there is no ''safety valve'' built into the play, the quarterback's ability to run to the outside could be his own salvation. If not, the cheerleaders go two-for-two on pass receptions.

THE "SPECIALS"

The ''Draw'' and ''Screen'' plays are a must to complement the running and passing games. They keep the defense honest. Each with proper execution, is designed, to turn a game around in your favor.

It may start out looking like a pass play, but once the handoff is made to the I-Back it's ''Draw'' all the way. The Draw play illustrated in Diagram 6-31 (b) is a bit different in that it uses a ''lead'' blocking back. The play can open anywhere from the center to the front-side tackle. It all

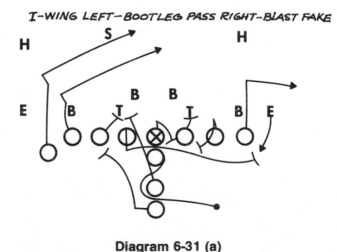

I-WING LEFT–BOOTLEG PASS RIGHT–BLAST FAKE

Diagram 6-31 (a)

depends on the charge of the defense. The linemen show modified "cup" protection and, instead of protecting inside, they give ground straight back while turning their man whichever way he wants to go. The lead back then picks up any garbage which has filtered through or broken loose as the ball carrier follows. Any uncovered lineman shows "cup" first and then doubles up on the nearest defensive man to the running area between center and tackle.

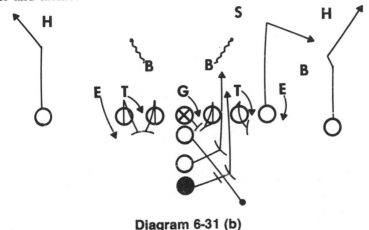

Diagram 6-31 (b)

Assuming that most secondary coverages will end up as three-deep arrangements, the widest receivers go "flag" to spread out the defensive halfbacks. The second receiver in tries to pull the safety to the outside by driving down on him and running an "out."

The guard-tackle splits can go out to four feet to open things up. However, the guards should split no more than two feet from the center. That makes it wide enough to invite the rush but narrow enough to handle it so the quarterback can get back and make the handoff.

Screen passes, which were once relatively easy to pull off, now require a gimmick or two to magnetize the rush men. The uncontrolled, stampeding rush, with the defensive linemen licking their chops and entertaining visions of interring the quarterback to his final reward are just about gone. In Diagram 6-32, the sideline screen is used with a fake draw to attract the rush to one side. After awhile, the left-side rush may become a bit leary about being burned by a phoney "Draw" and the next time around they'll be sure to be sniffing sideline "Screen." If that happens and the rush starts peeling off, then fake the sideline and dunk one over the middle. One simple assignment change involving the right end, in this case, brings into play a middle Screen off the action shown in Diagram 6-32. See Diagram 6-33.

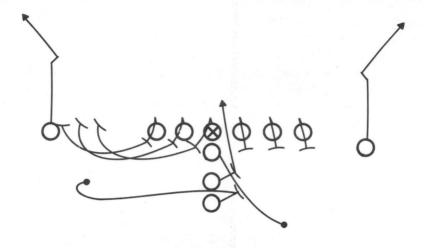

Diagram 6-32

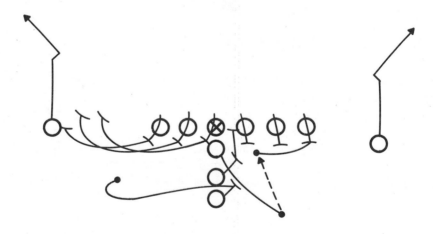

Diagram 6-33

On both Screens, the linemen hold for a 2-count before turning on the act of beaten pass protectors. The releasing linemen have designated areas and blocking responsibilities as they set up their wall of interference. "Outside-inside" is the general rule which is followed. The outside, or widest man in the screen, has outside responsibility first. If no pressure shows, he then looks upfield. The middle man, or second man out to the screen, checks downfield first and then looks back to the inside.

Inside is the center's only responsibility. Once the back has caught the ball and yells, "Go!" the screen heads downfield blocking their areas.

The fullback shows "Draw" and then seals off the center-guard seam just enough to make it look real and give the quarterback a chance to throw. A 1-count pass block is given by the I-Back before he slides out laterally behind the screen. If the call is a "Middle Screen," the end rolls behind the guard after making his 2-count block and sets up for the throw.

DRILLING FOR COORDINATED
SCREEN BLOCKING

How many times has a "screen man" been set up only to have a defender come streaking right by the so-called "wall" of blockers to put the "stick" on him? A dozen questions can be asked about what in the world were those blockers thinking about. "Didn't they see the guy? Where they standing around picking straws to see who was going to make the block? Don't those idiot coaches teach those kids anything?" All kinds of intelligent statements are made when a screen pass goes up in smoke.

An excellent drill for eliminating this particular catastrophe is shown in Diagram 6-34. It has several defenders, either live or with hand dummies, coming in hard from various directions. This forces the peeling linemen in the wall to exercise their "outside-inside" rule and, also gives them a good idea of about how much time they'll have to ready themselves for throwing their blocks.

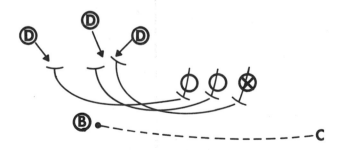

Diagram 6-34

There is a tremendous amount of material on passing that hasn't even been mentioned. Advocates of throwing the football will probably scoff at the limited amount of plays and patterns which have been presented. However, the basic attack covered in this chapter is more than adequate if the patterns are run properly, the protection holds up, and, of course, if the receiver hangs on to the ball.

Still to come are the goal-line passing attack in Chapter 7 and the two-minute offense in Chapter 8. The audible system is also included in Chapter 8.

The Polypotent Offense
Attacks the Goal Line

FROM THE FIVE IN

Nothing hurts more than to be shut out when you've had the ball first-and-goal on your opponent's five-yard line. Four plays can't get five lousy yards! It's a disgrace that you can't score when you're down so close in what is sometimes called "bleeding territory."

There are at least five possible areas which can account for this deficiency in offensive output. First, there is always the strong possibility of a breakdown in communication. A breakdown which can occur in the huddle, or in the exchange from a substitute entering the game to the quarterback, or from the coach originally giving the substitute the information. If a breakdown does result, there's going to be anywhere from · one to 11 players doing something wrong that will make the opposite 11 very enthused. Description in play calling and a uniform set of terms can tend to slice this type of error to a lean minimum.

A second type of mistake is the penalty for taking too much time. This is a stupid error. From first-and-five you're pushed back to first- and-ten. You're also out of your goal-line game plan. Again, communication in some form is usually the culprit. A slow decision or confusion under pressure on the part of the coach to get a play in from the sideline is the primary cause. And there's no excuse for this sort of blunder. Preparation, anticipation, and a play call which is concise and easily relayed erases this slip-up. Sending in plays in the goal-line situation should be practiced along with the goal-line offense. The head coach should not be on the practice field standing behind the offense. Instead, he should be on the sideline, near the team bench, sending in the game-plan plays. See

Diagram 7-1. He can also be reviewing game hand signals by flashing them to his quarterback if this type of communication system is used.

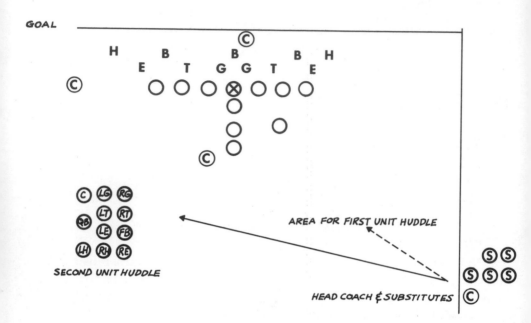

Diagram 7-1

The blown assignment is a third way to foul up a scoring chance. No matter how you look at it, poor coaching is to blame in 99 percent of the cases. A player who is hesitant or unsure down near the goal line is not prepared to play the game. This is the fault of the coach. There is, however, that rare occasion when each and everyone of us has had to call on someone from the bench who, mentally, is not playing with a full deck. Even though he's a nice kid, we all dread and fear this moment. Sure, we've tried to teach him to block the man in the opposite-colored shirt. Now we're fearful that he might crunch the guy in the black and white stripes. Only in this case are we, as coaches, absolved from any blame for "poor coaching."

Other types of penalties are a fourth way to stifle the offense. These usually come in the form of illegal motion or offsides. Why players take it on themselves to jump or move around and kill a scoring opportunity is an unanswerable question. However, answers are hunted. This is one reason why the goal-line offense is kept simple. There is no shifting; though it can be done. The formations are kept to a minimum. But, others are available. And, a limited number of set plays are practiced for when the ball gets on or inside the five-yard line.

And finally, there is lack of aggressiveness. Technically, it's not really a mistake but, if the offense is timid, the game's all over. If the offense isn't willing to "bleed," if the backs won't run through that proverbial wall, if they lie down and let the defense take it away, then they deserve to lose. An aggressive goal-line offense can be coached. However, it has to be coached with enthusiasm if it is to be a success. If you're the old nice guy on the goal line, then you can go into the locker room with your players and rationalize how you almost won the game. It simply boils down to a case of too many "if's" and not enough "hits."

GO WITH BLOCKING FORMATIONS

Back in Diagram 1-26, a variety of offensive formations were diagrammed for the general overall attack. The goal-line offense gets special treatment. In most cases, from the "five-on-in" the wide-open formations are shelved. Everyone is in tight to block and help punch the ball across that imaginary plane.

Three sets are generally used with the goal-line offense. These are the "T," "Stack," and "Full" and are drawn up again in Diagrams 7-2 (a), (b), and (c). These three formations allow the offense to attack the

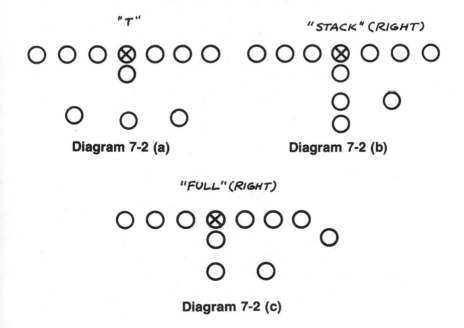

Diagram 7-2 (a)   Diagram 7-2 (b)

Diagram 7-2 (c)

areas of the defense with maximum blocking, minimum ball handling, and simple assignments. Yet, there is enough diversification in the plays to strike anywhere at the goal-line type of defense. It's no big military secret that once you get down to the five-yard line you can expect some version of either a "Gap-8," 6-5, or 7-4. You can also logically antici-pate gaps or shoulders being played by the front people on the defense. See Diagrams 7-3 (a), (b), and (c) for the goal-line defensive alignments.

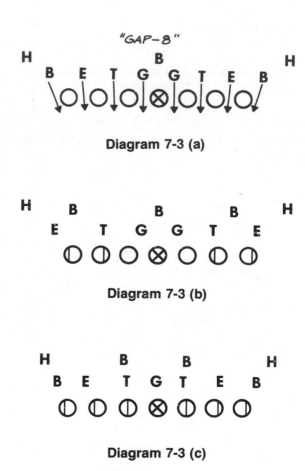

Diagram 7-3 (a)

Diagram 7-3 (b)

Diagram 7-3 (c)

There are five plays which make up the running portion of the goal-line offense. One for each of the five seams along the line from the center to the sideline. By limiting plays, formations, and assignments the number of possible mistakes is also minimized. Through constant repetition and practice against the probable goal-line defenses, the "Trap," "Wham," "Drive," "Keep," and "Sweep" are perfected.

Execution, coupled with simplicity, is the objective of the goal-line offense. The plays mentioned all have specific backfield actions which have previously been covered. Where the "Blast" had one "lead" blocker, the "Wham" is the same action run from "Stack" with two blockers in front of the ball. Even the quarterback's footwork has been boiled down to where he is using reverse pivot mechanics on each of the running plays.

The defensive combinations which are faced on the goal line are similar to those already analyzed. The big difference is there are 22 bodies in a relatively small area of the playing field. And these 22 bodies pump an amazing amount of adrenalin once that ball crosses the five-yard line. As a result, thinking isn't easiest thing to do, so blocking rules are kept nice and simple.

The goal-line offense has its own predetermined blocking assignments. No blocking calls are given in the huddle. If the name of the play such as, "Trap" or "Sweep" is called, those existing rules are used by the linemen. The quarterback uses the expression, "Goal Line" to precede the play call. This indicates that a minor blocking adjustment is to be used. These adjustments are mainly in techniques and involve the use of the "closedown" type of block to prevent penetration. These adjustments will be discussed with each individual play.

FIVE SEAMS TO ATTACK

Diagram 7-4 illustrates the points along the line of scrimmage which the goal-line offense will try to penetrate. Five running plays cover the

Diagram 7-4

field from center to sideline. True, there's no apparent running action coming back from formation strength but there's not that much need for it when you're only a yard or two out. The counter-action threat is there and must still be respected by the defense. Three formations and five running plays are variety enough to keep any defense honest. So what if their scouting reports show that you have tendencies to run certain goal-line plays. Your offensive charts have the same information. Let the guy across the field coach his players to anticipate certain plays. Set him up and then cross him up. Part of coaching strategy is baiting the other guy.

GAPS AND THE POLYPOTENT
INTERIOR TRAP

Here is where the quick, inside trap really comes in handy. Diagram 3-4 was an illustration of a pretty typical goal-line defensive arrangement with the center-guard gaps plugged and a middle linebacker playing on the heels of his down linemen. The entire picture of that defense and the goal-line trap blocking is shown in Diagram 7-5. The only blocking changes come from the outside where the ends are throwing closedown blocks to the inside to shield off any pursuit or, to seal off any penetration.

"GOAL LINE"-FULL RIGHT—SPEED TRAP LEFT

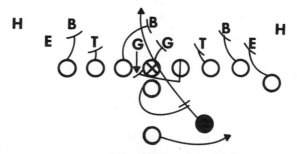

Diagram 7-5

The center and guard's rules for the interior trap were summed up in Chapter 3 as "Crack-Crack-Kick" with the back-side guard having a "gap" rule which had to be followed without exception. Inside the five, you're going to get gaps. If you don't, then invite them. Get the guards to split out to two feet. Make it tempting. At least get a gap charge from a head up man on the snap. A center-guard gap defense is the greatest thing in the whole wide world for the interior trap play. So, do everything short of begging the defense to honor your request for a gap alignment.

"Speed Trap" and "Buck Trap" are the two trap plays used. The "Speed Trap" is preferred because of the slanting action of the back and the "speed" at which the play hits. See Diagram 7-5. The "Buck Trap" from "Stack Right" is illustrated in Diagram 7-6 against the "Gap-8." On any of the goal-line running plays, the quarterback's only real concern is his call at the line of scrimmage. "Gaps!" between "Set" and "Ready" re-alert the linemen that there is indeed a gap defense in their play area. They may know it but they get the word just the same. Nothing is taken for granted when a six-pointer is so close.

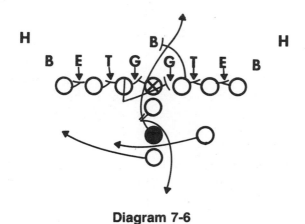

Diagram 7-6

"WHAMMING" THE GUARD-TACKLE SEAM

The "Blast" has one "lead" blocker. See Diagrams 2-1 through 2-3. The "Wham" has two. It is a short-yardage, battering ram type of play with special line blocking that is illustrated in Diagram 7-7. The "Stack Right-Wham Right" is drawn up against the 7-4 defense in Diagram 7-8. The backside of the line on the "Wham" is blocking to the inside. The closedown technique is used to cut off penetration. This rule extends to defenders both on or off the line as shown by the play of the back-side guard in Diagram 7-8.

The center is blocking the first man head on to his back-side gap. In no way does he block to the front side. The front-side guard has two choices in his read. These are labeled in Diagram 7-7. He has the man head on him first with his second choice being to the back side. If there is a man in his front-side gap, he ignores him. The front-side tackle picks up the man head on him or blocks the first man to his outside gap. His choices are also shown in Diagram 7-7. He also ignores any man lined up to his inside gap. If there is any man on the end, he is blocked to the outside. Otherwise, the end is using the closedown on the first man to his inside to prevent penetration.

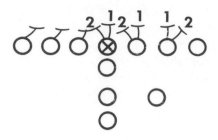

Diagram 7-7

As for line splits to the front side, it's minimal between center-guard and tackle-end. The guard-tackle seam should be opened up to at least three feet and even four if the linemen are quick enough.

The fullback and halfback are first of all responsible for any defender lined up in the guard-tackle gap. The defender can be either on or off the line and both possibilities have to be practiced. Most times, that man will be sitting right square in the seam. He can be off the line and hiding, as in Diagram 7-8, or he can be shading the tackle. In every case, it is the job

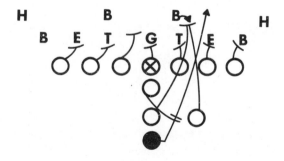

Diagram 7-8

of those two backs to blow him off the line. This is rough to do if the defender is down in a four-point with his nose two inches off the ground. It's even more difficult if he has been coached to maintain that low center of gravity while penetrating across low and hard. In this case, the backs just go "diving" into him with flying shoulder blocks thus creating a small pile and smothering the defender. The ball carrier then goes over the top the way he has been coached. See Chapter 10. Going over the top is true of any situation where submarine tactics are being used by the down linemen on the goal line defense. When they put their snoots in the ground and "hog" across low, this move has to be anticipated. Go over the top. If one back can smother the charge of the lineman and the other can "lead" the ball carrier over the top, then that's a lot of humanity for any filling linebacker to handle. Especially when they come flying at him in midair. This can be set up in a skeleton drill as shown in Diagram 7-9. If the guard or tackle lose their blocks, then the back to that particular side has to help out.

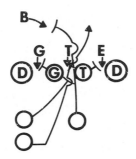

Diagram 7-9

THE POLYPOTENT "DRIVE" FROM "FULL"

The goal line "Drive" has the fullback going off tackle with a "lead" blocker. It is a play that was described in detail in the Chapter on "exception" blocking. However, there are no "exceptions" here. "Goal line," indicates the blocking call in the huddle and a possible "Gap" warning is given at the line of scrimmage. The ball is then snapped on a quick count. This is not the time to try and draw the defense offside or play games with shifts or men in motion. Hit people and score.

Blocking to the back side for the Drive is all closedown. To the front side, the guard and Tackle's priority starts with the inside gap and work to the outside. Their rule is strictly on-the-line and includes any man lined up "on." The end is also on-the-line conscious. He starts by looking to his inside gap and reads to his outside. Any linebacker on him or in his area is left for the lead halfback and possibly the wingback. The center takes on any man lined up on him who is on or off the line.

The real key to the Drive from Full is the watchdog block of the wingback. He is in position to really clean house on any linebacker in the off-tackle area. The Drive doesn't have to be run from Full, but couple the wingback's block with the halfback's lead and you come up with a lot of blocking power. The "Full Right-Drive Right" is illustrated in Diagram 7-10 (a) against the 6-5 defense and in Diagram 7-10 (b) against the Gap-8 defense to show the slight variation in blocking for the end and the lead halfback. Backfield mechanics and quarterback footwork are identical to those variations of the Drive play discussed in earlier chapters.

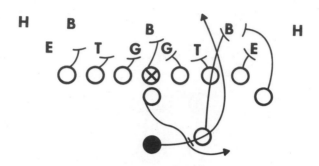

Diagram 7-10 (a)

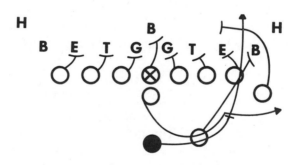

Diagram 7-10 (b)

FAKE THEM IN—THEN KEEP

There's something about pitching the ball inside the five-yard line that contributes to an ulcer condition. And this goes for either end of the field. Flipping the ball at the corner on the "Option" or "Pitch" is just asking for a fumble. There's not much sense in going to a finesse-type of play when the defense is really playing aggressively. This type of play is not abandoned. It still can be called. It's still in the play book. However, to get outside, the "Keep" or the "Sweep" is preferred.

Run it from "Stack," "T," or "Full." The "Keep" is an excellent play because of the good fullback fake off tackle. Add to this the fact that there is a lead back blocking for the quarterback and that the defense must still respect the threat of the trailing back from "Stack" or "T." The "Keep" is shown in Diagram 7-11 (a) against the Gap-8. It is also drawn up in Diagram 7-11 (b) to show the block of the wingback from a "Full Right" formation.

Back-side blocking for the line? "Closedown." What else? The center's assignment is the same as it was for the Drive. So is the front-side guard's. The front-side tackle still has a closedown block from inside to on but his rule has to be expanded to "on or off the line" since his man would be the stacked linebacker in a 7-4. It's not too far a reach to the first man from the tackle's outside shoulder because the end's split is one foot. He should be able to make his closedown without any trouble. His rule is enlarged to take in any man lined up on him either on or off the line. See Diagram 7-11 (a) and (b).

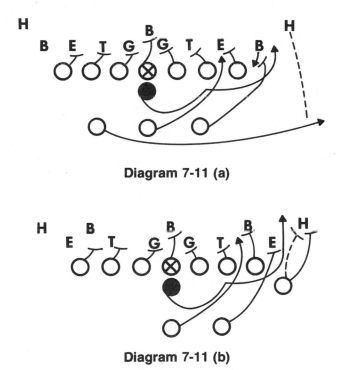

Diagram 7-11 (a)

Diagram 7-11 (b)

The quarterback and fullback must team up to try and draw the linebacker and end in with a good ride fake. This was shown in Diagram 2-13. The quarterback tries for the outside but if the defense shuts him off, then he should cut it up and get as much ground as he can. If he has a chance to sprint for the flag at the corner, then he should angle it out as fast as he can run. He should never bow his course back to get depth after the fake. This just contributes to the possible risk of losing yardage. He should think always forward never backward.

THE POLYPOTENT GOAL-LINE SWEEP

The play of the defensive corner on the goal line is such that it makes it difficult to use a kick-out to block anyone out in an effort to open up a running lane. The defensive ends are usually squeezing down hard thereby making it almost impossible for blockers to kick them out. So, the majority of work is done on trying to chop-in the corner when running the goal line Sweep. The ball carrier still reads his blocks but, in most cases, he can anticipate sprinting for the flag.

The goal-line Sweep can be either the "Pitch" or the "Give" as discussed in Chapter 5. Limited formations restrict the variety of Sweep calls which were enjoyed in the middle of the field. They do not however, curtail the effectiveness of the Sweep as a fine goal-line play. Two versions of the goal-line Sweep are illustrated in Diagrams 7-12 and 7-13. The play call is given with each of the diagrams.

The basic Sweep concept as previously defined has one small alteration on the goal line. Only one guard pulls. It has to be that way. There is just too much chance of front-side penetration if both guards pull out to lead. Another reason for keeping the front-side guard at home is that the halfback and fullback have better angles for the chop-in blocks which are being anticipated. Their blocking can be likened to the aggressive type of pass protection which they give on Sprint-out passes. This was discussed in Chapter 6.

STACK RIGHT — PITCH SWEEP RIGHT

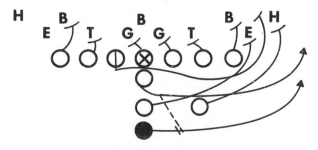

Diagram 7-12

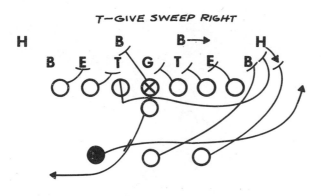

Diagram 7-13

With the back-side guard pulling out, the end and tackle have their option of using the closedown or the shut-off block to seal off the seams. The center has the first man to his back side. This is also the case for the front-side guard. He's using a closedown on the first man to his back side starting with the gap. The front-side tackle has a closedown assignment on any man on-the-line starting from his inside shoulder. Keep and Sweep assignments are identical for the front-side end. See Diagrams 7-11 (a) and (b) along with 7-12 and 7-13.

If the quarterback gets into the Sweep blocking because of the Pitch,'' his job is to lead the ball carrier to the Flag. He'll be with the back-side guard who has the task of curling up at the corner and trying to cut off linebacker pursuit.

POLYPOTENT GOAL-LINE
PLAY-ACTION PASSES

If the ball has to be thrown to try and score from short range, it will come off a play-action pass. There are five goal-line running plays and each one has its own action pass which includes the halfback throwing the ball from the Sweep. "Speed Pass," "Wham Pass," "Drive Pass," "Keep Pass," and "Sweep Pass" are the basic plays and they are supplemented by the "Bootleg Pass." They are illustrated with their set patterns in Diagrams 7-14 through 7-19.

The patterns for both ends are set on all of the goal line pass plays except the Bootleg. To the front side, it's a "flat" cut and to the back side, the end runs the "long post." There's not much room to get depth

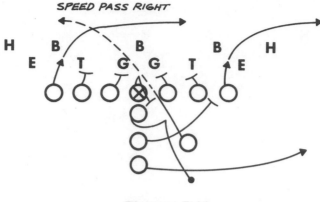

Diagram 7-14

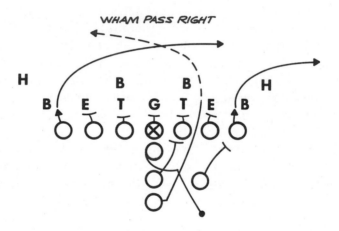

Diagram 7-15

and maneuver, so the receivers have got to cut across the field and try to get open. One technique which helps them get free is a solid one-count pop with a "brush block" before they try to run their routes. This tactic can cause a pass defender to misread his key momentarily and get him to think "run." A single moment is all that is needed to get free. On the Bootleg call, the receivers try to get out clean by avoiding the defenders. Pressure is put on the corner people by the run-pass threat of the quarterback. And the Bootleg is, indeed, a run-pass type of option play, with the quarterback setting his sights on that flag anytime he thinks he can get in.

Blocking up front is aggressive with the linemen reading from inside to outside. If the center comes up uncovered, he steps out at the

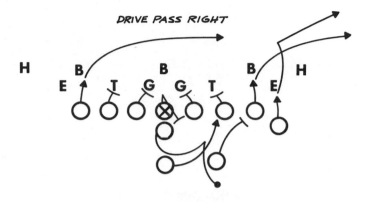

Diagram 7-16

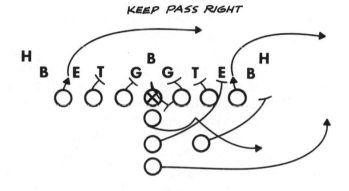

Diagram 7-17

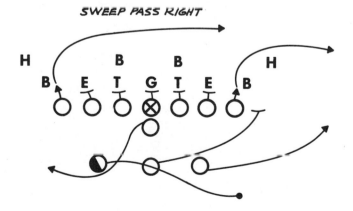

Diagram 7-18

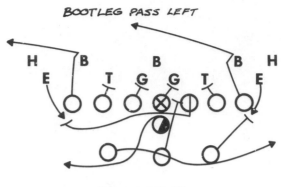

Diagram 7-19

linebacker and then backs off and looks to the back side for any rush. The backs are also blocking aggressively. Goal line is not the time to be passive. The action of the faking back has also got to be fast and hard so that he'll be tackled at the line. If awards are given out to be pasted on helmets, then any back who gets hammered at the line because of a good fake deserves a fistful of stars. Any faking back who does get through the line without being tackled should try to redeem himself by drifting into the back-side pattern. See the broken lines in Diagrams 7-14 and 7-15.

Diagram 7-1 in the beginning of the chapter, illustrated the practice setup for the goal-line offense. There's only one way to practice goal-line. You have to simulate what it's like inside the five. Even during the season, when the amount of contact in practice is kept to a minimum, goal-line offense is the time to get in your contact for the week. There are no excuses for not being able to come up with "five lousy yards in four plays!"

CHAPTER 8

Using Audibles and Specials
in the Polypotent Offense

TYPES OF AUDIBLES AND AUTOMATICS

Those skeptical of a no-numbering type of offense argue that audibles or an automatic change of plays at the line are too difficult to call and understand. There are no proven grounds which can support this negative viewpoint. And furthermore, it is much easier to translate descriptive codes or words than to perform mathematical calculations.

Many different audible systems have been dreamed-up and put into operation. Numbers, colors, and various code names have been used singly or in combinations to change plays at the line of scrimmage. There is really no best way to call an audible. The important thing is that if it fits into the system of communication and is understood by the members of the offensive unit then that's how automatics should be called.

Once a play has been called in the huddle, many different things can happen which can cause that play to be ineffective. These negative aspects, of course, are dictated by the opposing defense and the games that they play. Some of these roadblocks include finding the defense stacked in the hole where the play is supposed to go. The quarterback may find the defensive secondary pre-rotated into the area he had planned to throw the football. Linebackers planning to "dog" may tip their hands too soon and give the opportunity for a change of play. And, too, the defense can be it's own worst enemy and come up with a set which will make a play or even a good portion of the offense go if it can be called at the line, For example, a linebacker can "adjust" himself out of a play by going into double coverage on a split receiver. See the illustration in Diagram 8-1. This move has the possiblity of opening up a "Belly Blast" to the left side where the offense has the advantage of three blockers against two defenders. The play doesn't necessarily have to be the Blast. There are other calls available. The only limitations are how intricate and extensive the system of audibles should be for a particular game.

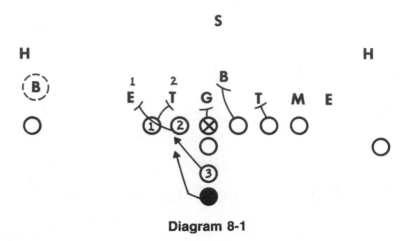

Diagram 8-1

An audible call at the line of scrimmage doesn't have to be elaborate or involve a mathematical translation. The example in Diagram 8-1 is as complex as the descriptive system can get. From whatever play was stated in the huddle, the audible to change it is: ''Blast-Lee-Fo!.'' The Blast play is run to the left (''Lee'') with ''Fo'' blocking. This is almost identical to the way the play would be called in the huddle. ''Lee'' is the only change and that, of course, is the code for left. ''Red'' is the right call.

A change in the blocking assignment for the front-side linemen is a very simple call. For example, the ''Roll Right'' as shown in Diagram 8-2 (a) could have been called in the huddle with zone-lead blocking. See

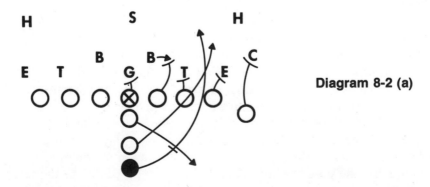

Diagram 8-2 (a)

Diagram 8-2. If the defense had aligned themselves as shown in the diagram, this would have been a difficult zone block for the linemen to make. If the quarterback can pick this up, he can change the blocking call to "X-lead!" for example, to create better blocking angles for the linemen and a more effective lead block by the fullback. This is shown to the front side only in Diagram 8-2 (b).

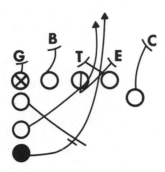

Diagram 8-2 (b)

In another case, the offense could wind up facing a "monster" set which could take away the "Belly Drive Left." See Diagram 8-3. The quarterback can switch the play from left to right away from the monster by calling out, "Red!-Red." When a play is changed from one side to the other, the call is repeated twice. This is because a one syllable word is being used and the repetition cuts down the chances of someone missing the audible.

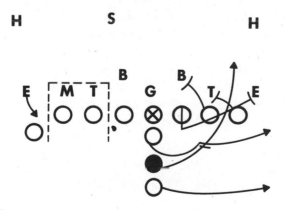

Diagram 8-3

Changing plays at the line is not limited to the running offense. Pass plays or an individual pass cut can also be audibled with little trouble. For example, let's say that the defensive secondary is playing back and that the linebackers are inside versus a formation with split receivers. See Diagram 8-4. Regardless of what type of play has been presented in the huddle, the quarterback can make the change at the line and unload a "Quick" pass to either one of his receivers. The audible is made by designating the side first and then the "Quick" cut. In Diagram 8-4, it would be called, "Lee-Quick!" Of course, you're not going to get away with too many "Lee-Quick" or "Red-Quicks" in a game. The guys across the line aren't dumb. However, a few false calls by the quarterback are sprinkled in to keep everybody honest and on their toes.

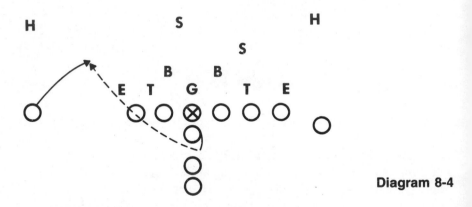

Diagram 8-4

These are but a few possible ways to take advantage of the defense. The big hang-up, of course, comes with the team being alert and with it's ability to make the change when the quarterback goes to the audible. The thinking processes have to grasp another play or blocking rule and make the adjustment or switch in a split second. Sometimes it works. Sometimes it doesn't. And this is the big disadvantage with audibles. However, a unique and understandable procedure of communication can eliminate many of the mistakes and blunders which are attached to the use of audibles.

THE GAME SPECIALS

The use of a special play for each opponent was mentioned in the discussion of the passing game. Since most teams play an eight-or nine-game schedule, nine special plays are presented and explained. They are described in common football terms. As mentioned, however, they can be given a special name for each particular team that will be faced. Depending on how accurate the scouting is in a particular league, some of these plays can be used more than once during the season. There are even a few specials which are set up in a series of two to three different plays from one look, motion, or formation.

The specials include both passes and reverses and really make the offense polypotent. They offer the advantages of being fun to practice; they generate enthusiasm among the players; and they are a great way to build confidence and morale by working on them at the end of each practice session. A touch of the razzle-dazzle can always perk up the squad and make them give more effort in the conditioning phase of the daily practice routine.

A version of the "End Around" is shown in Diagram 8-5 from an I-Wing formation. The end-around reverse is off the Belly Drive fake with the wingback handing the ball to the back-side end coming around. After the quarterback hands off the ball, he tries to block to the outside with the I-Back. The interior linemen use zone blocks to try and keep the defensive men occupied.

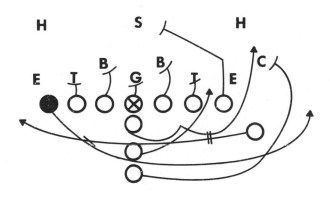

Diagram 8-5

If the end has the talent to run and throw, then a pass off the end-around reverse can be an excellent play. Even if he can't throw worth a lick, someone can be spot substituted to throw the ball on this play. A key? Maybe. See Diagram 8-6.

On both plays, the wingback has to cheat out and back to allow enough time for the quarterback-fullback fake before the handoff is made to him. The left halfback or I-Back has to chop the defensive end in while the quarterback provides additional protection to the outside. Both end-around reverses should have the end hesitating one count before he starts his path for the ball. He has the option of running or throwing on this play whereas the other end-around reverse was a straight run. The front-side end releases and runs a "flag." His pattern is lazy until he plants for the fake and cut. Then he takes off and looks for the ball.

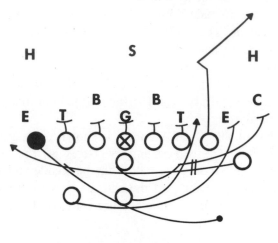

Diagram 8-6

It's as old as the "Lady" herself, but year after year the "Statue of Liberty" pops up in someone's football game. See Diagram 8-7. The key to this particular version of the Statue of Liberty is whether or not a back

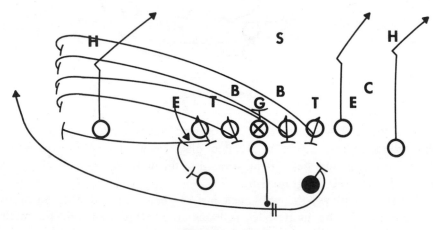

Diagram 8-7

can get a chop-in on the defensive end. On third-and-long-yardage situations the rush of the end is noted and sized up. If he can be "had," then this is as fine a special play that has ever been dreamed-up by a coach. The play is run from a spread set with the quarterback dropping straight back about seven yards while holding the ball chest high and looking to his right in this example. The back to his right shows pocket or "cup" protection, circles around tight, and takes the ball from the quarterback. All receivers make the breaks on their cuts away from the play. The interior linemen all show pass, hit for two counts and then curl across and downfield to set up a wall for the ball carrier.

It is also possible to throw a "Screen Pass" off the fake Statue of Liberty. Several different offensive sets can be used. The I-Wing formation is illustrated in Diagram 8-8 although the same "Pro" in Diagram 8-7 would make for a companion play to the Statue of Liberty. The "Statue Screen Right" is thrown to the wingback. Back-side blocking is "cup" while the center and front-side guard and tackle fire out hard for a one-count aggressive pass block. The front-side tackle then blocks out, the front-side Guard loops and looks in and the center leads.

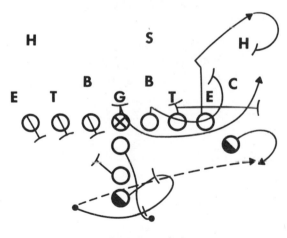

Diagram 8-8

A third play which can be run off the Statue of Liberty is a shovel pass to the wingback or flanker after faking the Statue of Liberty. This is shown in Diagram 8-9 from the I-Wing formation. The quarterback takes his seven yard drop and brings the ball back as he does on the Statue of Liberty play. He makes the fake to the halfback and then flips an underhand toss to the wingback coming across. The burden is on the halfback to carry out his fake well. As the fullback sets up to block, he watches the play of the defensive end. When the end reacts to the Statue of Liberty fake, the fullback blocks him with a kick-out and the wingback cuts up and through.

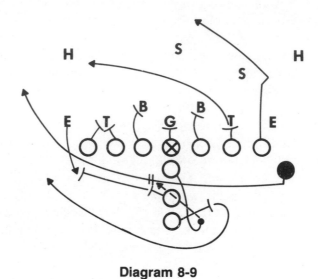

Diagram 8-9

The "Draw" play was illustrated back in Diagram 6-31 and is a reliable long-yardage situation play. To add some spice to the Draw, try the "Draw, Lateral and Pass." This play is shown in Diagram 8-10. The

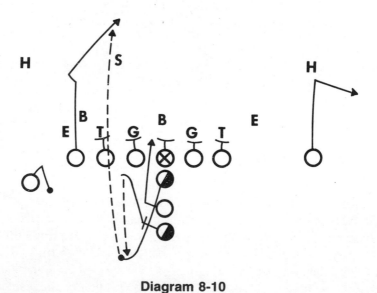

Diagram 8-10

quarterback takes a modified short sprint-out action as he hands the ball to the I-Back on the Draw portion of the play. After the I-Back gets the ball, he runs a course for the guard-tackle seam. When he is a yard in back of the line, he puts on the brakes, turns and laterals back to the quarterback, who lets one go deep to the left end. The end loafs through his drive downfield but turns on the speed as he makes his "post" cut when the I-Back pitches the ball back to the quarterback.

Another old-timer that makes it's appearance now and then during each season is the pass-and-lateral play known as the "Flea Flicker." See Diagram 8-11. A touch of "Slant" play-fake action is used to start the Flea Flicker. The quarterback rides the fullback one step and then throws to the end who is running a "hook." The end should have just enough time to turn to the outside and lateral to the left halfback or I-Back. In the illustration, the left Halfback takes a counter step for timing and to show "Slant" action before he fans out around the end. If the quarterback sees that the defensive halfback is covering the end too tight, he can drop back after the fake and throw to his right end on the "post" pattern. The importance of running a proper "hook" was emphasized in Chapter 6 and is repeated again. If the left end in this case drifts into the pass defender, he's dead and so is the "Flea."

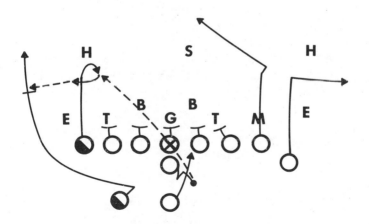

Diagram 8-11

If your opponent doesn't use a trailer to the back side, then the "Reverse" coming off the "Drive" fake is an excellent play for a third-down and long-yardage situation. The Drive and other Belly Series plays set up the Reverse. See Diagram 8-12. All the wingback does is run a deeper course than he would on the end-around play discussed earlier. His actions are the same. As the quarterback comes out of the fake, he flips the ball underhand to the wingback. The front-side tackle blocks zone and seals off penetration while the fake of the fullback occupies the end. All other interior linemen show ''cup'' protection and then curl around to set up the wall for the wingback. The halfback takes his counter step and anticipates a chop-in at the corner. If no trailer is in sight, he takes off and escorts the ball carrier.

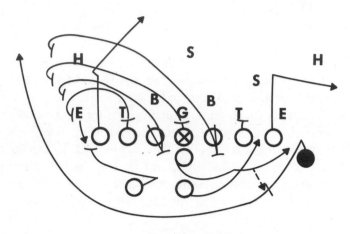

Diagram 8-12

The ''Out Reverse Pass'' resembles a ''Pitch Sweep'' at the start. See Diagram 8-13. The big difference is that the wingback does not come in motion before the snap of the ball. He starts out on the count and takes

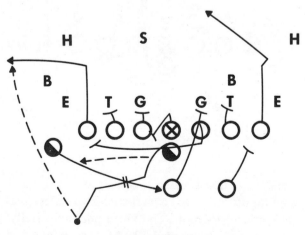

Diagram 8-13

the pitch from the quarterback. The quarterback begins the reverse pivot but deepens up slightly and goes for the wingback who hands the ball back to him. Once he gets the ball, the quarterback drops back and looks for the end to his side on an "out" cut. If he's covered, then he goes to the back-side end who is running a "post." The fullback fills for the guard who is pulling to protect at the corner for the quarterback. The halfback takes a shallow course to seal off any penetration from outside the tackle.

There's no limit to what the mind can dream up and create. The "Specials" which have been mentioned are merely a fraction of the plays which have, and can, come off a drawing board. They are an important part of the game, especially when they work.

THE POLYPOTENT TWO-MINUTE OFFENSE

Even before the entire team practices its two-minute offense, individual and small-unit work should be done in this area. Knowing the rules and keeping cool under pressure are probably the two most important aspects of manipulating time.

Much has been said about "milking-the-clock" and many methods have been used. A few ways in which the clock can appear to be standing still are the incomplete pass, a timeout, and the ball carrier going out of bounds. A first down stops it temporarily as does a penalty or an injury. Several plays can be called in succession to conserve time. A pre-arranged, pre-practiced no huddle offense can be ready for the closing minutes of a half or game. The important thing is that every player on the team should have confidence in its ability to move that football the length of the field in less than two minutes or, in some cases, a few seconds.

The two-minute offense has to be practiced. It has to be practiced against the clock. It has to be practiced with all the chaos that accompanies those closing moments of a contest. Set plays have to be ready. Series have to be ready. Last ditch gambles have to be ready. Nothing can be left to chance.

Drilling for the two-minute offense can be accomplished the same way in which the goal-line offense was practiced. This was discussed in Chapter 7 and illustrated in Diagram 7-1. If possible, have one or two assistants act as officials. Have a stopwatch on hand to count off the time if you don't have the advantage of a stadium clock. The offense should be informed of its timeouts remaining and the time left should be given whenever possible.

A controlled type of scrimmage is usually best for this type of work. There's no sense in losing a quarterback by adding too much realism. However, a good pass rush and a linebacker being fired every now and then won't hurt.

At the same time, a team must also know how and when to kill the clock to protect a lead and save a ball game. The important thing is knowing when to start. Going into a stall too soon could take the momentum away from the guy in front and give the other team the necessary shot in the arm they need to put points on the board. Common sense states stay in bounds, run wide plays which take more time, avoid excessive ball handling, don't throw, and take a maximum amount of time in the huddle once the ball has been spotted and made ready for play. Practice, though, is much better than relying on common sense.

PRACTICE AGAINST THE
UNUSUAL DEFENSE

The offense can always anticipate. It's hunches, however, are limited by scouting-report data and the past performances of the particular opponent. But any good defensive team will come out and toss a little something different at the offense. This can be anything from a stunt to an entirely unexpected alignment. The well-schooled offense will adjust and handle the ''unexpected'' because they've seen it before on the practice field.

You have to stay with the scouting report. However, it doesn't hurt to throw in an ''even'' set, for example, every fifth play of a scrimmage even though the defense is a straight, odd, five-man front.

Stunting is the one area which has to be worked against with each offensive practice session. It should be reviewed in drill work. It should be reviewed in skeleton scrimmage and live scrimmage. And, if feasible, one final look should be taken in the end zone during the pre-game warmup.

The primary reason for stunting is to confuse the offensive blocking. If a team gives only lip service in practice to blocking stunts, that particular squad will most certainly end up confused. So what if the scouts swear on a stack of Bibles that the week's opponent played it straight the whole game. Practice against the stunts.

The coach in charge of the prep team should have a number of different stunts drawn up on cards. These cards can be flashed to the defense to have them execute a certain maneuver. The stunts can be elaborate or a simple slant or common loop. But it is imperative that the offensive lineman get a different picture from that of a man lined up on his nose.

All of this takes time. And there's not a coach in the game who ever believes he really has enough time to get his team ready.

In preparing a team for a game, it is almost impossible to get more than two offensive units ready. Staff size, time, and lack of talent are three good reasons. Therefore, these teams should be picked with great care and the practice organized in such a way that the two units get the opportunity to run each play which has been scheduled for the particular game.

Watching is one thing, but participating and executing make for a better player. To give more players a chance to see some action in practice, two defensive prep teams should be shuffled in and out about every four plays. This results in 44 players being kept active and interested. Even the "spare parts" can be given their opportunity to show their stuff. They, too, have to be given the chance to show why they put that suit on day after day. And, even if it means their turning in that uniform, they have been taught the valuable lesson of being true and honest with themselves.

CHAPTER **9**

Coaching Polypotent Blocking

THE HOWS AND WHYS

In teaching blocking fundamentals, emphasis is placed not only on proper execution to the last detail, but also on the "whys." Eight chapters have stressed communication. And it doesn't stop here. The coach has to communicate with his players on all phases of the game. There is little blind acceptance, on the part of present-day youth, of the coach's ideas. The players want to know the "whys" of the game and it is the good coach who explains the rationale of a particular technique, play, strategy, conditioning drill, or training rule. The player's "why" is not due to rebellion but is curiosity. In most cases, it represents a genuine interest on a boy's part to learn more about the game. As coaches, we know it takes more than curiosity to survive the August double sessions. So, with the help of a little applied psychology, we can still run a program under the rules of an authoritarian, loving dictatorship.

Although there is no substitute for ability, aggressiveness, and desire, the "why" and execution are most important. Any coach who leaves uncorrected a poor stance, lazy take-off, a head down, a poor blocking surface, a narrow base, no leg drive, or any of the other items which go into a block is not coaching. These are faults, no matter how minute, which must be hammered away at in practice.

TEACHING THE POLYPOTENT BLOCKS

In Chapter 1, names were assigned to the various blocks which were to be used by the offense. The techniques and drills for developing these

157

blocks are now explained and illustrated by sequence pictures.[1]

There has been a trend over the last several years for many offenses to rely primarily on the face or butt type of blocking. The blockers fire straight out shooting their mask for their opponents' sternums and take them back off the line. This particular technique does not fit in with the theory of creating a running lane. See Diagrams 1-8 (a) and (b). The straight-ahead shoulder block is still favored even though the initial start of the block is similar to butt blocking. Many coaches will remember the days prior to the mandatory face mask and recall firing their face into a man and then sliding the face to the side. Strawberries on the cheeks was a lineman's battle decoration. The same beginning is followed with the "Zone" block. See Series 9-1: "Zone."

Photos 1 and 2—The blocker fires out from his stance, stepping with his right foot as he prepares to make contact with his head, right shoulder, and forearm.

Photo 3—Contact is made with a hit-and-lift motion attempted.

Photo 4—The turn portion of the block begins. Balance is maintained with the free left hand dropping down into a crab. The initial hitting surface with the right forearm is lost here, but the blocker keeps shoulder contact with continued leg drive and forcing his head back.

Photos 5, 6, 7, and 8—The blocker continues to turn and drive as he gets more of his head into the block. He still has contact and is turning on his man by staying with a wide base and using short choppy steps. Crabbing with both hands, i.e. "Scrambling," prevents his falling off the block.

The demonstration in Series 9-1 for the "Zone" block also illustrates the "Scramble" technique. Maintaining contact and keeping from falling to the ground are just two of the many important ingredients which make for the complete block. In the perfect Zone block, the blocker's hitting surface would stay firm and his free hand would go to the ground for the "crab" to maintain balance and drive. If the blocker starts to lose contact, then he goes to the four point position. The true Scramble was discussed in Chapter 6 in dealing with various types of pass protection.

Angle blocks are illustrated in Series 9-2 and 9-3 with the near and reverse shoulder types of blocks. The "Crackdown" block in Series 9-2 is shown with two linemen. If a wingback and a linebacker were used in the demonstration, then the blocking technique would be referred to as the

---

*All the photos in Chapter 9 appeared in *Athletic Journal*, April 1972, Vol. 52, No. 8, and are included with the permission of the publisher, John L. Griffith.

Series 9-1: "Zone"

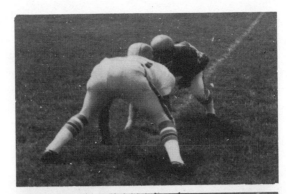

Photo 1

Photo 2

Photo 3

Photo 4

Photo 5

Photo 6

Photo 7

Photo 8

"Watchdog" block. The wingback would take a shallow course to the inside, almost scraping the tails of the defensive linemen, to hit the linebacker. This was drawn up in Diagrams 1-15 (a) and (b). See Series 9-2: "Crackdown."

Photos 1 and 2—The blocker steps with his inside foot, pointing the toe directly at the defensive man. His hips and shoulders should also be aimed directly at the defender.

Photo 3—Contact is made with the head and near shoulder as the right leg, in this case, is brought up for a wide driving base.

Photo 1   *Photo 2*   *Photo 3*

Photo 4   *Photo 5*   *Photo 6*

Series 9-2: "Crackdown"

Photos 4 and 5—The blocker aims for a target below the defender's shoulder pads. This is an ideal area to land a solid shot and maximize balance. The head is kept up to aid the blocker in staying with his man.

Photo 6—The far arm is whipped into the block thereby creating a broader hitting surface. Leg drive continues as the defensive man is ridden out of the play.

Prevent penetration. The expression has been used numerous times throughout the text to stress the importance of keeping an interior defensive man from getting into the offensive backfield. Series 9-3 shows the reverse shoulder or "Closedown" block. See Series 9-3. This type of block can be difficult to teach. For some reason, or reasons, players find it hard to shoot their heads across the front of the defensive people. They find keeping contact and maintaining their balance is tough. However, these, and a number of other problems, can be ironed out right at the very beginning with simple and functional drills and a lot of patience on the part of the coach. The teaching process will be covered later in the chapter.

Photos 1 and 2—As with the "Crackdown," the "Closedown" starts out the same. One important adjustment is made. The open step should be aimed well in front of the defensive man. This is done to insure that the blocker will make contact across the front of the defender.

Photos 3 and 4—The blocker shoots his head across the front of the defender and hits with his far shoulder. His feet are apart and his knees bent as the driving portion of the block is commenced.

Photos 5, 6, and 7—Defensive penetration is cut off by the blocker's head being in front. The blocker should fight to keep his head up because once he starts looking at grass he'll lose the block. Contact is maintained through good balance and leg drive.

Series 9-4 pictures the "Kick-out." It's the running shoulder block used on a defender by the offensive man coming from the inside to the outside. The shoulder to the side of the play is used as the blocker kicks his man out. The series shows a back using the kick-out on a defensive end. As we have seen in developing the offense, the kick-out can come from almost any back or interior lineman as was shown in Diagrams 1-12 (a) through (c). See Series 9-4: "Kick-out."

Photo 1—The back takes one step forward and at a slight angle to get into position. At the same time, his head and eyes zero in on the area where the defender is lined up.

Photo 1   *Photo 2*

Photo 3   *Photo 4*   *Photo 5*

Photo 6   *Photo 7*

Series 9-3: "Closedown"

Photo 2—By pivoting off his right foot, he starts to square himself with the defender.

Photos 3 and 4—The back strives for an inside-out position as he aims for the target.

Photos 5 and 6—Contact is made chest high with the outside shoulder. It is important that the blocker run through his man instead of trying to dive at him. A helpful coaching point here is to instruct the blockers that when going right on a kick-out, hit with the right. When going left, hit with the left.

Photo 1   Photo 2

Photo 3   Photo 4   Photo 5   Photo 6

Series 9-4: "Kick-out"

The same explanation can be carried through to the "Chop-in" block which is demonstrated in Series 9-5. That is, the block can come from either the line or the backfield as was shown in Diagrams 1-14 (a) and (b).

Photo 1—The blocker approaches the defensive man and works for an outside-in angle. His eyes are focused on the man's outside leg.

Photo 2—Striving to get his body pointed upfield, the blocker continues to reach for the outside position.

Photo 1   *Photo 2*   *Photo 3*

Photo 4   *Photo 5*   *Photo 6*

Series 9-5: "Chop-in"

Photos 3 and 4—Contact is made waist high and the block is maintained by the four-point crab. The blocker drives into the man and works to get his head pointed upfield.

Photos 5 and 6—The crabbing continues as the blocker jams his man to the inside. He keeps driving and turning on the man so as to screen him off from the designated route of the ball carrier.

In order to fill the gap developed by a pulling lineman, the "Shut-off" is employed by an adjacent man who shuffles to his inside. See Series 9-6. "Shut-off."

Photos 1 and 2—The offensive man moves laterally and does not go out after the defender. His first step is to the side and he keeps his shoulders parallel to the line of scrimmage. He pushes off with the outside foot and steps with the inside.

Photo 3—The second step brings the outside foot up to the inside. It is not a crossover.

Photo 1   *Photo 2*   *Photo 3*

Photo 4   *Photo 5*   *Photo 6*

Series 9-6: "Shut-off"

Photo 4—The third lateral step of the shut-off is with the inside foot. This positions the blocker in front of the defensive man.

Photos 5 and 6—The blocker gets good forward body lean and absorbs the charge of the defender. This prevents defensive penetration.

Series 9-7 and 9-8 show how the individual blocking skills are put into combinations for various play blocking calls in the offense. "Trap" in Series 9-7 shows the back-side guard making the short kick-out to the front side.

Photos 1 and 2—The trap man steps with his inside foot and starts to turn his hips and shoulders. His head and eyes are looking to the trap area.

Photos 3 and 4—As the second step is being made, the blocker has his target in sight and tries to get good inside-out position. This is a difficult movement since the play of the defensive man in some situations can make a picture kick-out difficult.

| Photo 1 | Photo 2 | Photo 3 |

| Photo 4 | Photo 5 | Photo 6 |

Series 9-7: "Trap"

Photos 5 and 6—Solid contact is made. The blocker's leg drive does not give out with the hit. Here is where live legs are needed to overpower and bury the defensive man.

For a review, go back to Chapter 3 where the entire "Trap" theory was explained in detail.

Cross blocking is an important part of the off-tackle portion of the offense and is shown in Series 9-8. The "X" blocking calls use the individual skills of the crackdown and kick-out.

Photos 1 and 2—The outside blocker starts with his basic crackdown footwork. Unlike the normal kick-out on a trap or wide play, the "X" block is a short, quick maneuver. The inside man steps laterally with his outside foot and looks for his block. This jab step allows the outside man to clear.

Photos 3 and 4—The outside man continues with his crackdown block while the inside man pushes off and angles up to his assignment.

Photo 1   Photo 2   Photo 3

Photo 4   Photo 5   Photo 6   Photo 7

Series 9-8: "Cross-Blocking"

Photos 5, 6, and 7—Following the rule: "Going right, hit right," the inside man kicks-out and follows through on his block.

FUNCTIONAL AND SIMPLE DRILLS

In teaching the individual blocking skills, a number of instructional methods are used. These include various demonstrations. form blocking, "by-the-numbers" blocking, half-speed work, and full go. Several different teaching aids are also employed and these include dummies and sleds.

Starting with the straight-ahead shoulder block (zone), the details and their whys are emphasized through constant reptition. Stance, start, head up, eyes on the target at all times, contact, proper breathing, full blocking surface, wide base, heels out, live legs, crab with the free hand to sustain contact, and block until the whistle blows are emphasized in every phase of instruction. From demonstration and form to live scrimmage, and then to the game itself, the goal is to execute, execute, execute.

The importance of a quick explosion and delivering a blow with a full hitting surface is worked on by using both the six-point and three-point lunges against the sled or stand-up dummies. Form and single blasts are used first followed by adding three rapid-fire shots. At first, these are under the command of the coach. Afterwards, a simple order to "hit" can start the multiple hit-and-recover blows of the drill. Emphasis is placed on leading with the wrist and forearm and not whipping the elbow. Swinging the elbow into the block can first of all possibly be picked up as being illegal by the official and second, it has a tendency to throw the blocker off center on his charge.

To develop balance, base, and drive, while still keeping in mind the other details, the board drill is used with stand-up dummies. See Diagram 9-1. The boards don't have to be fancy. Their function is to force the

Diagram 9-1

blockers to keep a wide base while they drive the dummies. The man holding the dummy also plays an important part in the drill. His resistance is controlled so that the blocker has to use force as he drives the bag down the board. Three tries with each shoulder is adequate work before moving on to the next phase of putting the zone block together.

Exaggerating the importance of turning the defender is shown by using the hit-and-turn drill on the stand-up dummy. See Diagram 9-2.

Diagram 9-2

Have two blockers, separated by the dummy, face each other in their offensive stance. On the count, they both fire out making contact with the same shoulder. They should turn on the bag as they drive against each other with the dummy sandwiched between them. Forcing against the dummy with their heads and necks, they maintain the crab position for a full revolution until they return to their starting position. A wide base and "live legs" are stressed in this drill along with quick movement. The two players are really competing against each other. If one lets up for just a fraction of a second, the other man will overpower him and end up on top of him and the dummy. The man on top must finish his complete revolution even after the cave-in happens and this can be an unpleasant experience for the bottom man.

Using the combination of boards and a modified hit-and-turn, place the dummies three-quarters of the way down the boards. The blockers fire out, make contact, drive and turn in one fluid motion, moving the defender out of the running lane. See Diagram 9-3.

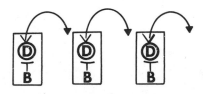

Diagram 9-3

Aside from demonstration, form, agility drills and the drills mentioned, stand-up dummies and sleds serve a limited function. Players do not have stationary targets to hit during the game. Drills, in order to serve a purpose, must resemble game conditions and the myriad of movement which takes place. The hand dummy gives the necessary flexibility and allows for the defensive man's action and reaction.

Using hand dummies, work continues on the zone block. The fire-out and modified hit-and-turn drills shown in Diagrams 9-1 and 9-3 are repeated with the hand dummies. More realism is then added to the drill work. Diagrams 9-4 (a) and (b) show drills using lateral pursuit and the spin-out techniques by the defensive man. As contact is made, the coach signals the direction of the maneuver to the defense. The first time these drills are used the majority of the blockers will lose contact because of a breakdown in any one of the details of the block. Three of the most common are the head goes down, no turn for body position, and failing to crab when falling off the block. See Diagrams 9-4 (a) and (b).

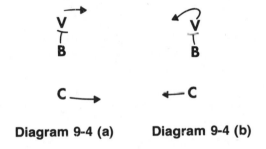

Diagram 9-4 (a)   **Diagram 9-4 (b)**

Live blocking is the real test so just drop the bags in the drills shown in Diagrams 9-4 (a) and (b). The most popular of all live-blocking drills is the 1-1 stall drill. Everyone gets a turn. Here is where the ball carriers learn to appreciate the work that's done for them in the so-called "pit." See Diagram 9-5. Later, they can be added along with other frills to carry the ball and make the combat more realistic. See Diagram 10-18 (a).

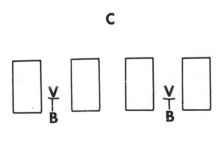

Diagram 9-5

The crackdown (Series 9-2) is taught by placing a defensive man in the gap. Hitting with the near arm and shoulder and getting the head behind are emphasized. The instruction comes in four steps, starting with form and progressing through hitting a stationary bell dummy, to the hand dummy and finally, live. As the blockers become more proficient, the amount of angle is varied to make the block more difficult. See Diagram 9-6.

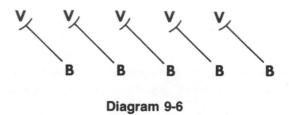

Diagram 9-6

Coming down on the first man inside, hitting him with the far arm and shoulder, and getting the head in front are the teaching points for the closedown (Series 9-3). The same four stages of instruction are employed in teaching this type of block. When movement is used, instruct the defensive men to fire across hard. Again, vary the distance of blocker to defender. See Diagram 9-7.

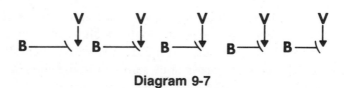

Diagram 9-7

With the zone, crackdown, and closedown covered, other blocks are added to expand the necessary skills needed by each of the positions. Many different drills have already been illustrated throughout the text as the various plays in the offense were described. Among these were several drills for the kick-out and the watchdog. The shut-off (Series 9-6) has been discussed and the alignment used in the sequence photographs is about as realistic as you can get for setting up a drill.

As we saw in Chapter 1, the term ''lead'' designated a fill block by a back at the area of attack as he picks up a linebacker or helps one of his linemen. This was illustrated in Diagrams 1-16 (a) and (b). Two drills which are helpful in teaching the backs how to block are shown in Diagrams 9-8 (a) and (b). When the ball is live, people don't usually stand around waiting to be hit. Therefore, in drilling for the lead block, moving targets are set up. As shown in Diagram 9-8 (a), the coach designates a number for the dummy holders before the count. When the blocker is about to hit the area of attack, the defender jumps into it. A variation is shown in Diagram 9-8 (b) in order to get blockers to pick up their feet when going through the line. Many times prone players prevent a man from carrying out his assignment. Two dummies are placed on the ground at the hole to represent this condition.

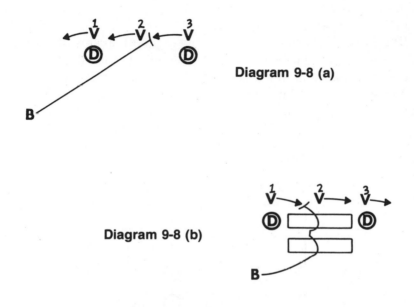

Diagram 9-8 (a)

Diagram 9-8 (b)

OFFENSIVE SLED DRILLS

If the ancient Chinese could coin a proverb pertaining to football, they would probably come up with something along the lines of: "One line coach is worth a thousand drills." This statement is not intended to offend those gentlemen whose job it is, day after day, to turn out skilled, tough, interior linemen. Darn good, loyal line coaches are an appreciated, rare commodity. However, a thousand sled drills are not used for developing offensive blocking fundamentals. Just a few.

The 7-man sled is a great piece of apparatus in that it enables a coach to get a lot of work out of a large number of players, in a short amount of time, with minimum supervision. It is ideal for form blocking. The players assume a right-shoulder block position, for example, on the pads of the sled. The coach makes the corrections. He checks for wide base, heels out, knees bent, tail lower than the shoulders, full hitting surface, free hand down in the crab position, bull neck, head up and hugging the pad. The next time they assume the shoulder block for form, they are instructed to start chopping their legs in place to get the feel of the balance steps and wide base. Two very common faults which can be corrected here are: (1) the legs seem to come together automatically and (2) there is a striding, pushing action with the legs instead of the short, choppy steps.

From this point, the stance and lunge can be added with the blockers springing out and holding the form. Then it's simply a matter of firing out, hitting, and driving at full speed.

The 7-man sled can be used to teach the short-trap kick-out block to a large number of linemen. Aligning themselves with their feet and shoulders perpendicular to the sled pads, i.e. facing to the side, they step with the near foot and hit with the same shoulder. They should line up about two yards from the pads and, as with all shoulder blocks, should make the contact a hit-and-lift motion as they drive the sled. See Diagram 9-9.

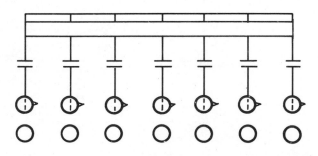

Diagram 9-9

Another excellent 7-man sled drill is the "Team Take-off." It is an outstanding conditioning drill and also provides practice in blocking and play running. Have as many offensive units as possible form their own huddles. The quarterbacks can call either the "Give Sweep" or the "Pitch Sweep" to the right or left. When its turn comes, each unit will break from the huddle, line up, and take off on the count. The backs run the Sweep action and the line will drive the sled, blocking with the shoulder opposite the call. When the backs clear the end of the sled and head up the field, the coach blows the whistle, ending the play. With the sound of the whistle, the seven linemen pop off the sled with a single handclap and a holler. Four or five units allow just enough time for the huddle to be formed, the players to catch their wind, and the next play to be called.

The 2-man sled is a fine piece of equipment for small unit work. Basic blocking skills and the kick-out for the short trap can be practiced. The only alteration which has to be made on the short trap is that the two blockers have to line up butt to butt so that they will both end up hitting with their inside shoulders.

Too often, players are satisfied with one hit and then they assume the role of cheerleader, spectator, or official signaling a first down or a score. They pat themselves on the back for a job well down while their ball carrier is being hit hard. Blocking until the whistle blows is used on all drills and the importance of hitting more than one man is shown in Diagram 9-10. Station two men with hand dummies behind each pad of a 2-man sled. Be sure they maintain at least a 10-yard interval while the sled is being driven. On the coach's signal, the blockers hip roll off the sled and sprint downfield throwing a running shoulder block into the first man and then using the opposite shoulder on the second man.

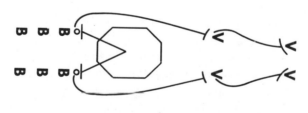

Diagram 9-10

POLYPOTENT DOWNFIELD BLOCKING

The biggest problem faced in downfield blocking is the fact that the blockers are dealing with a moving target. This is a difficult block to throw. It can be missed. It can result in a penalty. It can mean the difference between a win or a loss. In any event, downfield blocking has to be practiced. It has to be developed and put together just like any of the other types of blocks.

The initial drill for teaching downfield blocking stresses balance and the concept of a defender giving ground or backing away. See Diagram 9-11. Two large dummies are placed end to end about 5-7 yards from the line(s) of blockers. A defender with an air dummy straddles the prone bags about half way. In the early stages of practice, the blocker(s) jogs toward the defender, straddles the dummies, and places the crown of his helmet on the air dummy which is being held chest high. The next step is to have the defender back off just before the blocker makes contact. This forces the blocker to keep his head up and his eyes on the target. Speed is gradually increased and so is the impact of the block and the movement of the defender with the air dummy.

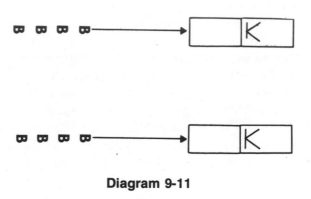

Diagram 9-11

To illustrate the pursuit angle or rotation of the secondary, a two-man defensive backfield is set up in the drill shown in Diagram 9-12. The blockers have got to learn to realize that they have to head off the defender. They have to lead him when they throw their block and the only time they leave their feet is when the defender is coming at them hard. Then they chop him down with a cross body block. Otherwise, they are taught to run through the defensive man and occupy him. In Diagram 9-12, the blockers are stationed along side the goal posts. Two defensive backs are set up about 7-9 yards off the blockers and about 1-3 yards outside of them. The coach signals the direction of the rotation and then gives the snap count. Unlike a play called in the huddle, the blockers in this drill have to read the flow of the pursuit or the rotation and adjust their course to the defender on the move.

BLOCKING ON KICK RETURNS

This section is not a discussion on types of kickoff or punt returns. Instead, it is a series of comments made in an attempt to correct faults that lead to missed blocks and, worse yet, a touchdown called back because of

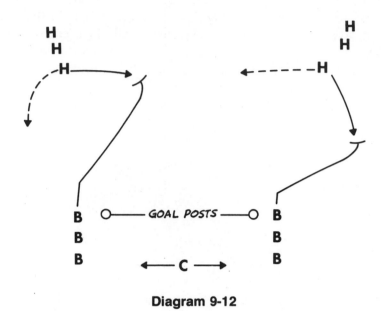

Diagram 9-12

a stupid "clip." The greatest waste of practice time is to review kick returns without the presence of tacklers whether live or dummy. There's just no possible way that a player is going to learn how to block for the kicking game by "shadow boxing" or pretending to hit someone.

When 22 people line up for the kickoff you can be assured that someone is going to get hit. But why in the heck does it always have to be the poor ball carrier before he even gets started. He can at least be given the opportunity to gain a few yards and get the ball into better field position for the offense to operate. One sure way to accomplish this is to practice the kickoff return against the full kicking team. Give them dummys and turn them loose. Let the players on the kickoff return team practice blocking against the "Suicide Squad." It's no easy task. However, a little practice will get that ball farther up field come game time.

The same is true of setting up the so-called "wall" on the punt return. Send coverage people down under the kick and have them try to crash the wall or sneak around behind it. The other team is going to try and pull it off. So be prepared. Even if you're holding your last practice session the day before a game, have people cover the kicks with dummies and give the players on the return team that one extra chance to perfect their assignment and skills.

Every coach has his pet drills. Those mentioned in this chapter have been successful and fit in well with developing the particular types of blocking fundamentals which are essential for the productivity of the offense. At all times, functional and realistic drills are used in the football program and they are in a continuous process of analysis and improvement. This is also expressed in the next chapter on backfield drill work.

CHAPTER 10

Developing the
Polypotent Running Back

IT'S NOT AS EASY AS IT LOOKS

Blocking is the crucial phase of offensive fundamentals and this is one fact which can never be refuted. Getting the man with the ball to take advantage of his blockers' efforts is another chore which faces the coach.

It is rumored that Jim Brown, the ex-Cleveland Browns great, once stated, "Anybody can run outside but it takes a Back to run inside." There's a lot of truth and meaning to that so-called statement. Therefore, a great number of skills must be taught in the process of developing a high school running back or, for that matter, any ball carrier. These, of course, supplement the natural abilities already possessed by the athlete.

DRILLS TO SIMULATE THE GAME

Assuming that the raw material available to the coach consists of average athletic talent, the process of making a back begins. Drills are a valuable teaching aid. However, drills which simulate actual game conditions and situations must be prepared and organized. Any other routines, unless they have a specific positive purpose, waste precious field time. For example, the popular forward roll is an excellent agility drill. But for a ball carrier? Once he hits the ground, the whistle blows and the play is dead. Therefore, the use of functional drills is imperative.

179

CARRYING AND CHANGING THE BALL

Ball carrying, change, and running skills are the first items taught. Diagram 10-1 is a convenient alignment for teaching ball carrying and running techniques. Saturation televising of football has proved to be a helpful visual aid in developing young players. But the professionals and collegians have also instilled a number of super-bad habits. Waving the ball around like the proverbial loaf of bread or spiking it to the ground both after and before crossing the goal line may excite the fans, but fumbles and turnovers lose games. And one day, some kid is going to be mighty red-faced when he gets nailed doing his "victory shuffle" before he has crossed the goal line. Carrying the football and protecting it is paramount in importance for the back. With the point of the ball snug at the arm pit and the hand and fingers firm over the front tip of the ball, it is protected both from blind side and back butts.

The football adage of keeping the body between the ball and the tackler is not important to some coaches. They prefer not to have their backs changing the ball. "Juggling" it from hand to hand will only lead to the ball carrier coughing it up. On the other hand, keeping the ball in the hand to the side line the back is running helps protect against the ball being jolted free by helmets of the pursuit. To change the ball in the open field, or when cutting back across the grain, the ball is brought across the front of the body. The free hand and arm go underneath with the ball being firmly grasped before it is switched to the opposite side. Carrying and change are taught easily and quickly from the alignment in Diagram 10-1.

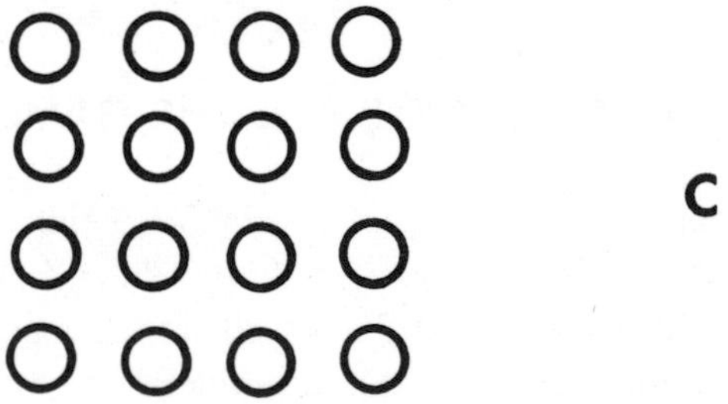

O O O O
O O O O   C
O O O O
O O O O

Diagram 10-1

"LIVE LEGS" FOR
RUNNING WITH THE BALL

As the late, former Head Coach of the University of Illinois, Bob Zuppke, used to say to his ball carriers many years ago, "Twist, turn, lunge, plunge, but keep going." Balance, cutting, live legs, and protection of the ball carrier himself are the next skills which must be acquired. The four-column arrangement from Diagram 10-1 is still maintained, but the coach moves off to one side. A series of drills is used to practice running with the ball. These drills are illustrated in Diagrams 10-2 through 10-7 and are explained by "Series."

Series A—Wide base and high knees: Diagram 10-2. To learn the importance of a wide base and to stress balance, the backs jog for ten yards with their feet slightly wider than shoulder width. They exaggerate the lift of the knees and keep their feet pointed straight ahead. The lines jog up and back changing the hand of the ball on the return trip

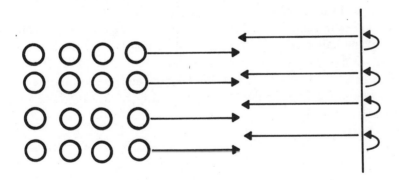

Diagram 10-2

Series B—Spinning: Diagram 10-3. Many times, as a ball carrier gets hit or creased from the side, he fights the force of the impact which has caused him to turn, stumbles, and falls. Instead, he should use the momentum caused by the blow to his advantage. Keeping the legs churning and continuing with the spin is easier than fighting pressure. Again, a wide base is stressed in the drill with high knee action. The spin is made as a four-to-five yard distance both up and back. On the return, the ball carrier spins in the opposite direction.

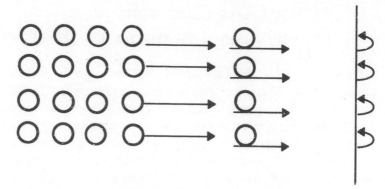

Diagram 10-3

Series C—Breaking the Fall: Diagram 10-4. More and more backs have taken to using their free arms and hands to break a fall after being tripped up. They regain their balance and make a substantial gain or even score, when it first appeared they would be down. This useful aid is easily taught. With the ball in the right hand, the back jogs about four yards and falls forward using his free arm and hand to break the fall without allowing his knees to touch. His forward motion wil! be confusing at first and many of the ball carriers will be unable to break their fall. Soon he will get used to having his legs "catch up" with him as he partially pivots on his free hand, and he will regain his balance and jog for another four to five. Change the ball on the way back and gradually increase speed as proficiency increases.

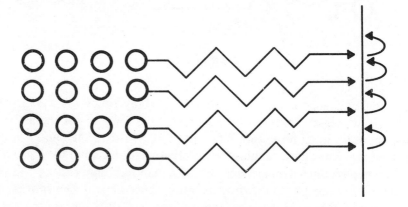

Diagram 10-4

Series D—The Forearm for Protection: Diagram 10-5. The first man in each line should be placed 4-5 yards in front of each row to represent a tackler. For half speed and demonstration purposes, no dummies are needed. For the full impact, hand dummies should be added. As the ball carrier approaches, have the dummy holder take a step up to meet him. At this point of impact, the back delivers a blow with his forearm. The upper arm and shoulder can also be added for protection. It should be stressed here, especially to those backs who are more aggressive, that their job is to gain yardage and cross the goal line. Some players misinterpret "protection" for going out of their way to club a defender. Destroying the tackler by running into him is not their primary objective. Evade, keep going, and protect is what they have to be taught. The forearm and pivot will be added later to help them accomplish these basics.

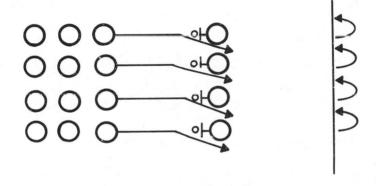

Diagram 10-5

Series E—The Vanishing Stiff Arm: Diagram 10-6. It may be ancient but it's still an effective way to get by a tackler. To practice the stiff arm and cross over step combination, have the first man in each line move out four to five yards. They should put their hands on their knees and be sure to lock their elbows in tight and bull their necks as if in a two-point stance. The top of the helmet is presented as a target so the ball carrier can stiff arm and cut off by shoving away with a crossover step.

Series F—Cutting: Diagram 10 7. By spreading out the lines, the backs can practice cutting. They should be instructed not to get carried away with "dancing" or faking in place, or the defensive pursuit may catch up with them and put an end to their budding careers as Fred Astaire Dance Studio instructors.

Once the routines in Series A-F are learned, they take only a few minutes of practice time. These are valuable, individual running skills and should be practiced as much as possible.

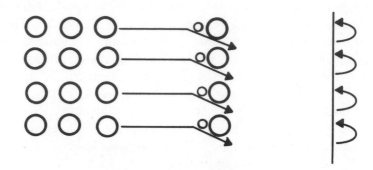

Diagram 10-6

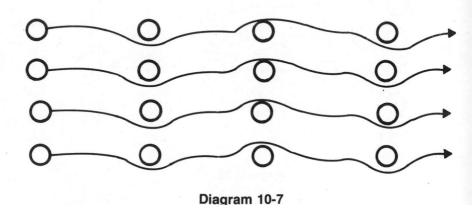

Diagram 10-7

THE RUNNING ROPES

When a blade of grass reaches up to tackle the ball carrier, then the offense is in big trouble. The running ropes, whether commercial or homemade, offer an excellent device in teaching running, agility, ball carrying, and change. Above all, they force the back to pick up his feet. The ropes are preferred over tires, which have a tendency to play havoc with the ankles. There are four drills illustrated in Diagrams 10-8 (a) through (d). These drills utilize no more than five to seven minutes of time and give each player the opportunity to go through the drills both at half speed and full tilt. Changing the ball can be practiced in all the drills except the ''sprint'' in Diagram 10-8 (d). As the players reach the half-way point, they use the proper technique for changing the ball. The players should also force themselves to keep their eyes up so they gain confidence in their running. In Diagram 10-8 (d), the players back off about five yards to get a good running start for their sprint through the ropes.

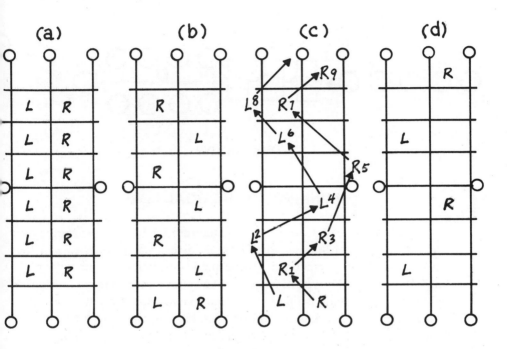

Diagram 10-8

EXPLODING AT THE HOLE

Diagram 10-9 is the Gauntlet and this is where the backs start to learn how to run inside. This drill offers variation while helping to teach balance, live legs, spinning, ball carrying and ''explosion'' as the back hits the hole. Three dummies are placed on the ground followed by two rows of backs. The first man on each side of the line delivers a forearm blow with his inside arm as the back hits the hole. This can be done with or without air dummies. The remaining players grab for the ball but do not step into the running lane. Pulling and pushing for the ball can cause the ball carrier to lose his balance. This is where he should employ the use of the "spin" to keep going. Another man is placed at the end of the Gauntlet with an air dummy. The ball carrier throws a forearm into him. A substitute dummy holder is in line, waiting to step in to speed up the rotation as the players work their way through the lines to become the ball carrier. It is very important that all the players get work and a chance to develop their basic running skills.

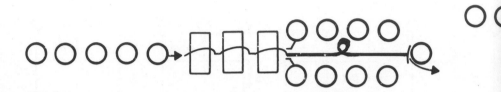

Diagram 10-9

RUNNING TO THE GOAL LINE

The forearm-and-pivot is used in Diagram 10-10. The psychology of running to the goal line has already been discussed. Here is one of the ways in which it is practiced. Three men are stationed with either air dummies or the taller type of stand-up bags about three to four yards apart and on an angle relationship of six to four to two yards from the goal line. Two lines can be used as illustrated. The back to the right hits with his right forearm and does a complete pivot. He keeps his legs going as he blasts each defender in succession as he works to run to the goal line.

THE POLYPOTENT GOAL-LINE DRILL

The value of live legs, drive, and going over the top can be practiced in what is called the "Goal-Line Drill." This is illustrated in Diagram 10-11. It is a good, competitive drill that many players find to be fun. Backs can go against backs or line against backs. The Goal-Line Drill provides a variation and welcome relief to possible practice monotony and drudgery by being a great morale builder. Five to seven stand-up dummies are stacked a yard from the goal line. They act as a buffer zone to prevent injury and represent the congestion encountered at the goal line. A ball carrier is placed three yards from the dummies. Three defen-

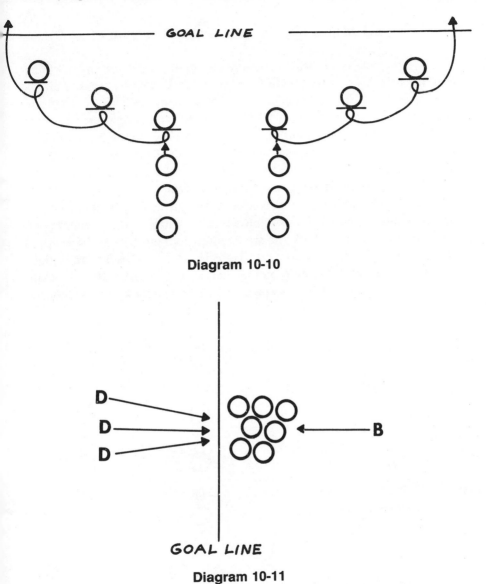

Diagram 10-10

Diagram 10-11

ders are lined up in a football position four yards from the goal line in the end zone. On the coaches' signal, the ball carrier attempts to score by going only through or over. The defenders try to stack him up and prevent the score. After a couple of attempts at the goal line, backs soon learn the importance of protecting the ball, utilizing running skills, and being a competitor. A quarterback can be added to the drill to practice handoffs and to add more realism.

LOOKING TO THE HOLE ON THE START

Whether it be the two,-three,- or four-point stance or any combination, the offensive stance and initial play starts should be practiced almost as a daily ritual. These areas are worked on from the basic four-column alignment shown in Diagram 10-1. From the particular stance for each position, each start(s) should be gone over by progressing from an initial step, to a jog, to the full speed running of the correct route(s). In Diagram 10-12, the halfbacks work on the Sweep, the fullbacks on the Drive, the I-Backs on Blast, and the quarterbacks on Slant.

Work on stance and start is accomplished, at first, without using a ball. It's much easier for a coach to correct mistakes which might come up. Common faults to look for are leaning, looking before the snap, or altering boot position or footwork. Here is where the backs are initially instructed to look to the hole on the snap so they can see their blocking develop immediately. It's just a matter of "step and look" in one motion.

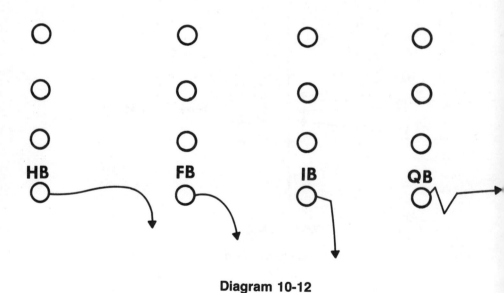

Diagram 10-12

RECEIVING THE HANDOFF

There are many different ways for a ball carrier to take the handoff from the quarterback. Take it with the hands is one. Another is to place the inside arm (nearest the quarterback) up and the outside hand at the side to prevent the ball from being pushed through and by the ball carrier. A third, is to place the inside arm up and the outside arm across the belt with the palm up to form a ''pocket.'' If the ''pocket'' idea is used, the thumb of the top hand should be turned so that it is pointing down. This little adjustment prevents the inside elbow from dropping down to shut off the pocket. Once this ill is cured, the amount of fumbles can be reduced to almost nil.

In the initial stage of teaching handoffs, two lines are used in an old, but effective, drill. This teaching aid was originally picked up from George Allen's *''Complete Book of Winning Football Drills''* back in 1959.[1] This is an excellent drill which allows for continuous repetition and makes feasible the supervision and instruction of a large number of players. See Diagram 10-13 (a). The backs should concentrate on hand and arm position, receiving the ball and clamping down on it without looking. After several tries from the right-hand side, the lines are reversed. Speed should be kept under control at first and then gradually increased. The lines can also be spread apart so that the backs can pitch the ball back and forth to get the feel of another form of reception—handling the dead-ball pitch. This is shown in Diagram 10-13 (b).

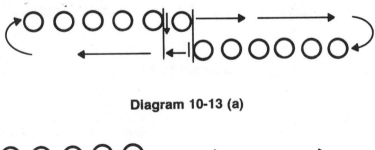

Diagram 10-13 (a)

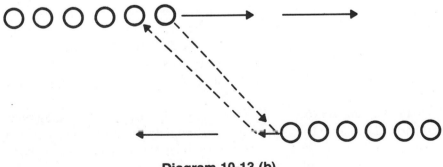

Diagram 10-13 (b)

[1]Englewood Cliffs, N.J.: Prentice-Hall, Inc., 1959.

Next, the quarterback gets added to the picture. In Diagram 10-14, four units are used to introduce the backs to receiving the ball from the quarterback on a handoff. The simple "Dive" play is used. Usually, the most common errors to appear at first are the back looking for the ball, reaching for it, and running on an angle to the quarterback instead of at the hole. Quarterbacks also make mistakes. Some have a tendency to use a sweeping motion in trying to get the ball into the pocket. They should slide it straight out. Too, if they can't reach the handoff, some will throw the ball at the back in panic as he shoots by. They should be instructed to hang on and follow the back into the line if the handoff is missed and, at least, gain a couple of yards.

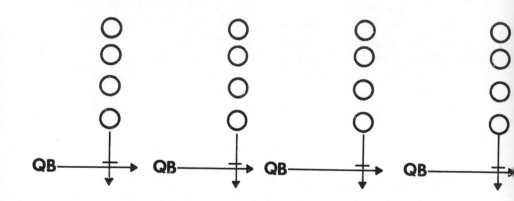

Diagram 10-14

Variations in stance, play starts, play routes, "head and eyes to the hole," handoffs and ball carrying are reviewed on a rotating basis as shown in Diagram 10-15. The quarterbacks rotate through the four plays illustrated, for example, to practice their footwork. Halfbacks and I-Backs can also switch positions to work on several different plays such as Give Sweep, Speed Trap and Blast. The fullbacks are working on the Buck Trap.

In Diagram 10-16, bell dummies are placed as obstacles and markers for particular plays. Other players are stationed with air dummies which gives the effect of the Gauntlet only with more realism. This type of arrangement permits play practice, ball carrying and running skills to be perfected. The fullbacks, I-Backs and halfbacks in Diagram 10-16, for example, get to work on the Drive, Blast and Slant.

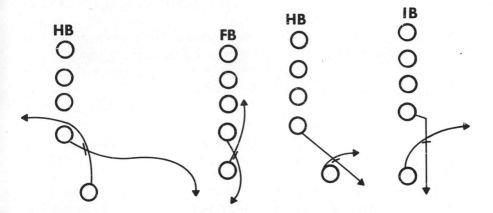

Diagram 10-15

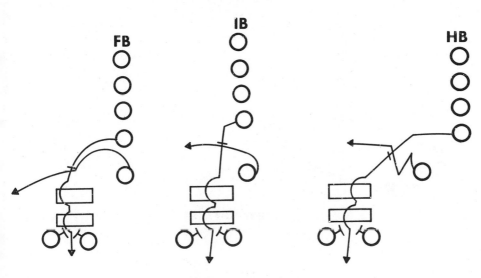

Diagram 10-16

AGAIN, RUN TO THE GOAL LINE

Numerous expressions have been coined to instruct backs on how to run with the football. This, of course, includes the now immortalized, "Run to Daylight."[2] Another axiom to follow is the previously men-

---

[2]Lombardi, Vince and W.C. Heinz, *Run to Daylight*, Englewood Cliffs, N.J.: Prentice-Hall, Inc., 1963.

tioned, ''Run to the Goal Line.'' An inexperienced back, and many times even the varsity starter, will run like a streak for the sideline if an interior hole doesn't open. He travels 40 yards laterally and gains nothing. And too many times he is rewarded with a not-too-friendly shove out of bounds by the not-too-friendly members of the defense who would like to see him end up in the third row of the stands.

The advantages of running to the goal line are: (a) it makes the back conscious of gaining yardage by heading up field, (b) it gives the back more options for cutting or breaking back across the grain, and (c) by facing the goal line, the back is square to the line of scrimmage and in a better position to protect himself from any shots by linebackers coming from the sides. This is illustrated in Diagram 10-17 (a). The only times that there should be a variation in this rule is when a play is specifically designed for a slant to the sideline or when the ball carrier has a good angle to the flag for a score. This is shown in Diagram 10-17 (b).

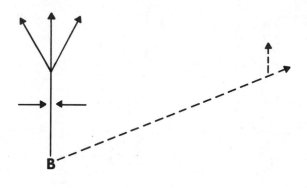

Diagram 10-17 (a)

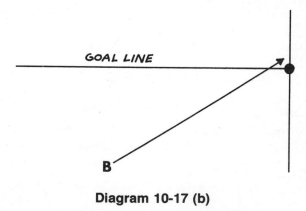

Diagram 10-17 (b)

FOLLOWING THE BLOCKER'S HEAD

The 1-1 stall drill has always been an excellent sorter of competitors from "football players." It is also very useful in working on and developing some of the finer points of carrying the ball. When using the 1-1 stall drill, there is an important and constructive piece of advice which can be passed along to the backs. Have them read their blocker's head and, if possible, run to that side. The rationale behind this is that the blocker's neck and head act as a shield and make it more difficult for the defensive man to destroy the block and slide off to make the tackle. He may get a hand on the back but, he shouldn't be able to bring him down with an arm tackle. This is illustrated in Diagram 10-18 (a). Variations of "reading the head" are illustrated in Diagrams 10-18 (b) and (c). In both cases, the back tries to set up the defender with a fake to make an easier block for his interference. Diagram 10-18 (b) shows the back giving a dip fake to the inside to get the corner to commit himself in. The back then cuts to the outside and his blocker takes the corner with a chop-in. The opposite is true in the next illustration where the fake is made out and the back cuts up inside the kick-out block. Both of these are typical Sweep play maneuvers. See Diagram 10-18 (c) and Chapter 5.

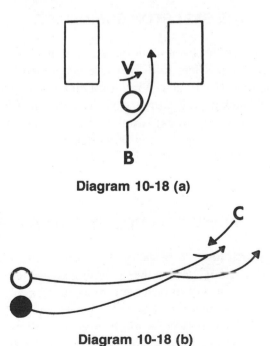

Diagram 10-18 (a)

Diagram 10-18 (b)

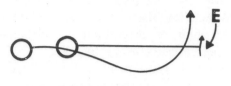

Diagram 10-18 (c)

IS FAKING AN IGNORED ART?

If there is any one element in a play outside of a good block which can make or break it, a well-executed fake is that ingredient. A good fake helps make the play go. This has been stressed time and time again in just about every chapter because it is so important to the success of the offense. The drills in Diagrams 10-14 through 10-16 can also be set up to practice faking. If faking is really an ignored art, it is because it is given only token lip service on the practice field and is not stressed.

THE SKELETON SCRIMMAGE

Every skill which has been mentioned can be reviewed and polished in a skeleton scrimmage. Here, too, is where assignments and timing are practiced. In Diagram 10-19, an I-Wing formation is set up to work on the "Roll Right" off-tackle play which was discussed in Chapter 4. This same type of drill was used to explain the "Belly Blast" and was drawn up in Diagram 2-5. The whole idea is to get one more defender than blocker into the scrimmage so that the back can work on his open-field techniques.

THE MAKING OF A POLYPOTENT BACK

The skills which have to be learned are numerous indeed but they can be taught and mastered. When these running skills are combined with the ability to block, you not only have a running back and blocker, but you have a football competitor. The young man who wears this badge gets his football uniform dirty by working over football players. He may not be gifted with natural athletic ability or physical size and blinding speed, but he'll deliver for you. And, he's not worried about playing the game with "owies" and "ouchies." He wants to play. This rare specimen of humanity makes coaching this game a pleasure.

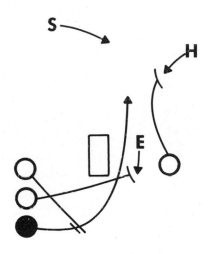

Diagram 10-19

A Final Word From The Author

Bud Wilkinson, while speaking at a coaches' clinic, was reported to have made the following statement: "Everything new in football can be found in the library. . . .Stagg did it all before 1900." I believe this to be true.

The consistent success of any football team is not achieved by gimmicks. Of course, talent is an important ingredient for winning but there are many teams which come up with respectable records and their share of the spoils year after year with average players. Every season there are those same teams which give you fits. They don't have a great thrower. They don't have a great back. They don't have great size. Yet they win and everyone wonders why.

In my opinion, there are four areas which are necessary for that annual above-the-.500-record. These are things which I was shown by others. These are things which I discovered on my own through trial and error. These are things which have contributed to any success that I have enjoyed as a coach.

There is but one trait that I would look for in a man whom I would work for, or with, in football. Loyalty is that trait. A coach must possess it. A staff must thrive on it. Second-guessers, bum-rappers, and back-stabbers, unfortunately, are also in this business. They don't last, but they cause their share of damage. And worse than that, their selfish lunacy ends up hurting the heart of this game—the kids. If a man is loyal, it doesn't make a bit of difference whether he learned his football from a book. He will be a good coach. He will be an enthusiastic coach. He will be an asset to the program. He will live and die with you and your school. And, he'll help you win.

Even though we are experienced coaches, all of us at one time or another need a reminder in two important areas. First, we must always remember that we are dealing with the adolescent athlete. He is going through the maturation process. He is developing physically, mentally, emotionally, and socially and sometimes his developmental growth can create all types of problems. Besides being a coach, we end up as fathers, confessors, counselors, and disciplinarians. Second, it is always easier for us to be a helluva lot tougher as a coach than we were as a player. Football is a fierce game. Yet, that young man has to be respected. He can be made tough without abuse.

Finally, the game is still, and always will be, one of fundamentals and execution. This is my belief. This is my philosophy. This is the reason for this book. Enjoy it. Use it. Criticize it. If it stimulates some thinking about this beautiful game, then it's a success.

INDEX